CREDIT SCORE REPAIR

DISCOVER THE BEST CREDIT SECRETS TO
EASILY FIX YOUR CREDIT SCORE.
USE PROVEN STRATEGIES EXPLAINED IN
DETAIL, AND LEARN HOW TO INCREASE
RATING AND MANAGE YOUR MONEY
BETTER.

Matt Bloomberg

2

Table of Contents

Introduction

A credit score is simply a rank of your creditworthiness with a goal number. In the past, if you need credit, you would have to go into the bank, and if you had a decent remaining in the network, or if the advance official had a positive sentiment about you, you could get an advance. However, there is a blemish in that framework; anyone can have bad credit despite their very much regarded. Along these lines, by computing the impact of various factors on your capacity to reimburse, the credit offices concocted a way that tries to treat everyone decently.

Not having a good credit rating can come with problems that can be dangerous. However, with exemplary efforts to get the best credit rating you can earn, you shouldn't worry for too long. Knowing what you are getting out of your cards and how they work is critical to your success regarding covering those cards and keeping them from costing more to use than you can afford.

Learning about credit and finance can be an intimidating task. I believe one should seek to understand anything they choose to participate in. We don't choose when it comes to credit, so why not have the knowledge and understanding of it regardless of any trade or career you are in or will pursue? Credit can always be used as a leverage tool, no matter how much money you have or make. Pay attention to how wealthy people secure mortgages to purchase their property and pay interest while still building equity.

Still, to truly live a happy life, you need to make sure that you are financially stable. This is done by saving money, getting your credit in good shape, and eliminating debt. Credit repair is a great solution for those needing to fix their bad credit. Understanding how it works can be tough, so the goal here is to provide good information accessible to everyone and viable solutions for people with bad credit.

This book contains proven steps and strategies for saving money and getting yourself in better financial shape. It can help you identify what you can do to get a better credit rating for your life. Many things that come with your credit are beneficial to your score. You can figure out what you can do to improve your credit score based on what factors go into it and how it affects your life. This book also provides actionable steps and strategies to improve your credit score quickly and take full control of your financial life.

The details on what you can do to manage your credit are varied. You can use many sensible strategies for managing your credit while using the right decisions. You can also get in touch with credit reporting bureaus to fix any problems you have with your report. You might not have to spend more money than what you are trying to cover on your credit profile. That is, you don't have to contact some outside credit repair group that would not do much of anything to help you. Most importantly, you will not have to worry about such a credit repair group ripping you off with the false belief that you could get some real credit help from that entity.

Of course, you might be doing a good job managing your credit, but if your identity is stolen, it could take a huge hit. This guide also explains how to fix your credit rating if you've been the victim of identity theft. This is a legitimate issue that has become increasingly prevalent around the world. As a result, it would be beneficial to look for ways to resolve your credit-related problems after being the victim of identity theft.

The details you will come across in this guide will help you resolve the many problems you might encounter regarding your credit rating. Be sure to see what this guide offers to find that it is not overly complex for you to get the most out of improving your credit.

Chapter 1. The Benefits of Having a Good Credit Score

All About Your Credit Score

Before we can do much about our credit and ensure that it is no longer low and causing us issues, we have to learn more about our credit score. There are a few different scores available that we can look through, and each one will rely on a different algorithm to determine how high or low your score is. However, the score that we need to concentrate on is the FICO score. This is the one that most people who will offer you money as a loan will look at, so it makes sense that this is the one that we want to focus on.

Do not assume your credit report is 100% accurate. The creditors who report data about your credit accounts to the credit bureaus are not always accurate in their reporting. If there is an inaccuracy or discrepancy in your credit profile, it could have a vastly negative effect on your credit rating.

How often do you check your credit report? You are entitled to one free inspection of your credit report per year. Unfortunately, most people don't take advantage of this opportunity. They will go years without checking their credit reports. But that is a bad thing to do because inaccuracies in a credit profile could be holding you back from a better job or bigger loan.

Everyone has a responsibility to know what is in their credit profile. You may request your credit profile from any of the three main credit bureaus in the United States. They must follow various state and federal laws about credit reports' handling and distribution.

According to the Fair Credit Reporting Act, the credit bureaus must investigate any credit disputes filed. If you discover a piece of information in your credit report that you believe to be false, you must file a dispute with that particular credit bureau and explain the problem to them.

Their investigators will review your dispute to see if it is valid. If they determine it is valid, the inaccuracy will be removed from your credit report, which will ultimately affect your credit score for the better.

Creditors must similarly follow state and federal laws too. The only difference is they aren't required to validate the data they report to the credit bureaus. That is the responsibility of you as the credit account holder.

Introducing of Credit Bureau and How Do They Work

The Three Primary Credit Bureaus

The three primary credit bureaus in the United States are Equifax, Experian, and Trans Union. They are also referred to as CRAs, which stands for Consumer Reporting Agencies. There is a fourth credit bureau called Innovis, but most creditors do not even bother reporting. Only the first three credit bureaus are essential to them for reporting purposes.

If you attempt to retrieve your credit report from any of these credit bureaus, make sure you retrieve it from them directly. There are third-party companies that gather consumer information and sell it to consumers who want to see their information. Don't waste your money on that because you can get your credit information from the credit bureaus for free.

Let's explore the different credit bureaus available.

Equifax

In 1898, Equifax was created by two brothers named Guy Woolford and Cator Woolford. It was the very first credit bureau ever to be established. Since its creation, Equifax has grown into the world's biggest credit bureau.

Since there had never been a credit bureau before 1898, the business's idea was revolutionary. Cator Woolford had run a grocery business up until that point. This business required him to collect sensitive information about his customers to ensure their credit was good.

Cator figured that other businesses would probably want to verify their customers' credit. So, he came up with the idea of selling his customers' credit profiles to other merchants. His original thought was that he'd make enough money doing this side business to cover his grocery business expenses. But, to his surprise, the business of selling consumer information became more profitable than his grocery business.

Cator got in touch with his brother, Guy, an attorney. The two of them planned to drive this business to a higher level. They formed the Retail Credit Company in Atlanta, Georgia, in 1898. The company targeted local grocery stores throughout Atlanta as their primary customers.

In the 1900s, Retail Credit Company expanded its target audience to the insurance industry. Over the 20th century, they expanded their services even further to banks, credit card companies, car dealerships, colleges, and other financial institutions.

In the 1960s, Retail Credit Company was already the largest credit bureau in existence. They had about 300 active branches across the United States. The type of information they collected from consumers had expanded as well. In addition to collecting their names, addresses, and employment information, they also collected information about people's childhoods and marital status.

Retail Credit Company started to put their consumer information onto computers to handle all this new information and their growing list of consumers on file. Not only did this make storing consumer data easier to do, but it also allowed Retail Credit Company to share the information more easily with other companies paying to receive it.

By 1971, Retail Credit Company captured the interest of the federal government. Too many people complained their personal information was being sold without their consent. In response, the United States Congress passed legislation called the Fair Credit Reporting Act. The first law passed regulated how credit bureaus could gather and sell consumer information.

Retail Credit Company had trouble obeying the new law during the first few years after it passed. This forced the government to pass more regulations and restrictions. For instance, credit bureau employees could no longer receive bonus payments for collecting negative information about consumers. It had been done a lot in the past, unfortunately.

By 1979, the Retail Credit Company's reputation was virtually destroyed. As the company attempted to change its ways and build a better reputation, its leaders thought it would be wise to change its name to Equifax. The name is short for "Equitable Factual Information."

Under a new brand name, Equifax took off in the 1980s. It was an active competition with Experian and Trans Union, as they all purchased smaller credit agencies and acquired their consumer files. Equifax was the biggest of the three, as they aligned themselves with at least 65 credit bureaus to grow their database.

In 1999, Equifax started selling credit monitoring services to consumers for the first time. It was around the time when identity theft became more common in society. Credit monitoring services were marketed to consumers as a way for them to check their credit and ensure no one was using their information to take out loans.

Equifax now has more than 401 million credit records of consumers from all over the world. Their headquarters continues to be in Atlanta, but they have operations in 14 different nations.

Trans Union

In 1968, Union Tank Car Company created a holding company by the name of Trans Union. This was 70 years after Equifax was created. Trans Union was not originally a credit bureau until it acquired the Credit Bureau of Cook County in 1969, just one year after its formation. Since then, Trans Union has been an active participant in the credit industry.

Trans Union did not start as a recognized credit bureau, though. It gradually grew popular over many years by purchasing credit bureaus in major cities across the country. The company believed that a national credit database would better serve creditors and consumers.

Credit companies used to be local companies in major cities. Their consumer records were nothing more than filing cards in a cabinet drawer. But after Trans Union acquired the Credit Bureau of Cook County and several other city credit bureaus, they transferred the data on those file cards to their national database.

In 2002, Trans Union bought True Credit. It allowed them to sell credit information directly to consumers for the first time. Ever since then, their business became even more successful. They have more than 249 offices across the United States and other offices in 25 nations globally.

Experian

In 1968, a major automotive electronics company named TRW Inc. had purchased another business called Credit Data. Quickly following the acquisition, TRW formed a TRW Information Systems and Services Inc subsidiary. It would be the original name of their future company, Experian.

TRW Inc. had been around since 1901, under Cleveland Cap Screw Company's name. It manufactured screws and bolts for automobiles and airplanes. As it started manufacturing additional parts and accessories, it became a massive company in the United States.

By the 1960s, the company started selling more than automotive and electronic parts. They were now gathering and selling consumer data too. It was what eventually led to TRW Information Systems' formation in 1968. They collected credit information from their customers and information from Credit Data.

Over the next 20 years, TRW Information Systems had millions of consumer data files on record. In 1986, TRW became the first credit agency to directly sell consumer data to consumers. They were way ahead of the other credit agencies in this endeavor.

Unfortunately, TRW experienced a series of setbacks in 1991. Thousands of consumers found that their credit reports had several inaccuracies and incorrect information on them, mostly concerning tax liens that were not real. The cases were resolved

15

over time after several consumers sued TRW. The company settled all the cases without going to a civil trial.

TRW was determined to stay in the credit business and get things managed better. They developed a new database called CRIS (Constituent Relations Information Systems). Without any more errors or issues, TRW was valuable once again. In 1996, private investors paid more than $1 billion to purchase ownership of TRW. After that, the investors purchased the biggest credit agency in the United Kingdom too.

Once all the credit files from both agencies were merged, TRW changed its name to Experian. It has continued to have that name over the last 24 years now. During this time, Experian has expanded its credit monitoring services to consumers in more than 65 nations globally.

Innovis

In 1970, Associated Credit Bureaus was formed. It went through a series of name changes over the next two decades after various organizations purchased it. It was renamed to Consumers Credit Associates in 1989 and then renamed again to Innovis in 1997. It has kept that name ever since.

Despite Innovis not being considered one of the three main credit bureaus, it made history the first credit reporting agency to capture consumer data and store it into databases automatically. But compared to the other credit bureaus, Innovis is still a relatively new credit reporting agency.

After all, Equifax has been collecting consumer information and selling it for over 100 years. Equifax, Trans Union, and Experian have hundreds of millions of consumer credit files on record. Most lenders and financial companies must not report credit information to Innovis.

In 2001, however, there was a breakthrough for the company after Freddie Mac and Fannie Mae required mortgage companies to start reporting credit information to Innovis. Still, it remains in the shadows of the other three credit agencies.

What Is FICO Score

First, we need to take a look at what the FICO score is all about. This is a three-digit number based on the different information found on your credit reports. It is going to help lenders figure out the likelihood that you will repay a loan or not. This, in turn, will affect how much you are allowed to borrow, how many months they will give you to repay, and how much you will pay in interest rates or the cost of the loan to you.

Any time that you decide to apply for credit, lenders need to find some manner that is fast and consistent with deciding whether it is a good idea to loan out some money to you in the first place. And it is pretty much guaranteed that they're going to take a look at your FICO score.

Not only does this kind of score helps lenders and more make decisions that are faster and smarter about whom they will loan money out, but it is also going to help most consumers get fair and fast access to credit when they need it the most. Because these scores are going to be calculated based on the credit information that pertains to you, you can influence your score if you make sure that you don't carry on too much debt, you pay all of your bills on time, and you ensure that all of your choices are smart for your credit.

About 30 years ago, the FICO or the Fair Isaac Corporation debuted these scores to provide a good industry standard for scoring how creditworthy each consumer was. This was meant to be a system that was fair to both consumers and lenders. Before this score, though, there were many different scores, and all of them had different methods of calculating how good your score was. Some of these factored in things like political affiliation or gender as well.

The FICO score has found a way to make this a much easier process to work with. Everyone is on equal footing when they start, and then the decisions they make about how much to borrow if they make payments on time, and more, will be what factor into the final score that they get. This makes it fair for both institutions and consumers to rely on along the way.

How the Scores Are Divided Up

There are several ways that we can take a look at the credit score that comes from FICO. In general, a lender will find that a score above 670 is a good sign of creditworthiness. The higher you can get your score, the more luck you are getting loans because you are seen as a lower risk, and you will likely be able to get more loaned out, depending on a few other factors like your income. A good idea of how these credit scores work with FICO includes:

1. Under 580: This means that you have a poor credit score. This is well below the average that most consumers in the

US will have, and it shows the lender that you are a risky borrower to give money to.

2. 580 to 669. This means that you have a fair credit score. This score is still below the average for consumers in the US, though it is possible to find some lenders to give out money, especially if you are at the higher end of this range.

3. 670 to 739. This is a good rating for credit score. This will fall near and sometimes a bit above the average for the consumer in America. This is the score that most lenders will feel comfortable lending money to.

4. 740 to 799: This is the range where your score is seen as really good. Your score will be above the average and show others that you are a dependable borrower they can trust.

5. 800+: This means that you have an exceptional credit rating. Your score will be well above what is considered average, and you can show off with this score that you are an exceptional borrower who will pay them back.

Why Is the FICO Score So Important

There are a lot of benefits to working with the FICO score. These scores have helped many millions of people gain access to credit for education, cover their medical expenses, and even purchase their first homes. Even some utility and insurance companies will check FICO scores when they decide to set up some of the terms of doing service with them.

The fact of the matter is that having a good FICO score can save you a lot of money in fees and interest along the way because if you have a higher score, it is likely that lenders are going to offer you lower interest rates on the money they lend out. This is because they feel that you present less risk to them than others.

An overall, quick, fair, predictive, and consistent score will help make sure that the cost of credit to everyone is going to be lower. When the lenders know that their risk is lower and do not have to worry about people defaulting along the way, they are more likely to offer lower interest rates to those who are using them and can ensure that we never have to pay more than necessary.

The more accessible credit in general is, the more lenders will be willing to loan out, and the more efficient they are going to be in some of the processes they use to drive down costs and pass those savings over to their borrowers.

The Difference Between FICO and Other Credit Score

Another question that you may have along the way is the differences between the FICO score and the other credit scores; some are out there. To get started, these scores are the only ones that the Fair Isaac Corporation creates, and they are used by about 90 percent of the top lenders when it is time to make lending decisions overall.

The reason for this is that FICO scores will be seen as the standard when it comes to making fair and accurate decisions about an individual's creditworthiness. They have come in handy to help millions of people get the credit they need for many different purposes.

20

There are other credit scores out there, and they can be used in some situations. These other scores will calculate the number they give you differently than the FICO score can. So while it may seem like some of those other scores are similar to what we see with the FICO score, they aren't. Only FICO scores will be used by most of the top lenders you want to borrow from, and while the others can be good for some monitoring of your score, if you would like, the best way to go is with the FICO score.

Chapter 2. How Credit Score Is Calculated

The credit score is calculated using several pieces of your credit report. If you want to have a high credit score or have good credit, you must know how it is calculated and what factors (banks and credit agencies) must approve or deny a loan or credit card.

Your credit score is calculated based on these categories, namely:

- The amounts that you owe

- The history of Payment

- What types of open accounts you have

- The age of the accounts

- The number of credit applications

Let's examine these factors and see how we can raise your credit score one by one.

The Amounts That You Owe

It is no coincidence that the amounts you owe are the next thing to discuss. This is because, after the history of payment, it is known to be the next most influencing factor of your credit score.

It is already a general rule that you are required to use only 30% of the credit the bank approves and nothing more than that. It will be highly unwise if you use all the credit that the bank approves, say $300 on a $1000 credit card. That means you should never make use of the maximum account allowed on your card.

Credit bureaus perceive this as an omen when you start to depend on the money, and they tend to withdraw as it signifies a negative mark for your credit report and your credit score.

I would advise you to use below 30% of your credit, or what's best is you could go ahead to use only 10% of your credit line and nothing more than that. By doing this, you will have better credit scores, and your chances of increasing and even sustaining a good credit score will be limitless.

The amount of money you owe is also a key factor to consider when calculating your score.

The History of Payment

Consider making payments on or even earlier than the agreed time, as it is absolutely important and has a major impact on your score. If you make late payments, then your credit score will dramatically reduce.

The fundamental thing a lender would want to find out is whether or not you paid your bills or even your credit loans in good time. This category, out of the others, majorly influences your credit score and makes up to 35% of your score, which is why it is very important to take note of it.

Now that you know that delayed payments can affect your credit score and hinder you from building a good credit history, you must ensure you pay all debts on time without any qualms.

The types of accounts normally considered for payment history are namely:

- Installment Loans

- Credit Cards (such as Visa, Master Card, and so on)

- Loans to the consumer

- Retail accounts and;

- Mortgage Loans

Remember, making and building a good credit score is a path that will require you to make payments on time.

What Types Of Open Accounts You Have

Another factor that can favor your credit score is having various types of loans (mortgages, cars, and student loans) and credit cards.

Your credit score is majorly concerned with the different types of credit you use, some of which exist are credit cards, mortgage loans, installment loans, and accounts with finance companies.

Note that it is not so important that you use each one of them, and I'll advise that you only open accounts that you are going to use.

The credit mix has no major effect on your credit score, but it is of great importance that your credit report does not contain excess information on which your score is based.

There is no perfect version of a credit mix as it varies with time from individual to individual. Opening car loans, student loans, and credit cards you won't be needing won't be advisable for you.

It would be an added advantage to have this factor that shows that you know how to handle your credit responsibly.

The Age of the Accounts

Consistency is key in the credit score world. As long as you keep maintaining a good credit score history, your credit score will always remain high. The general rule explains it as the longer you have credit cards, the more your credit score increases. That's why I'll advise you to start your credit as soon as you can. This is a factor that constitutes about 15% of your credit score, measuring the length at which you have your credit accounts and how well you have managed them within that period.

Here is what your FICO credit score records:

- It considers the age of both the new and old accounts and even the average age of all of your accounts.

- It also considers your credit lines (if you have), how long you have been with them and how your payment history has been.

- Finally, it measures your loans/credit cards' exact age. Because of this, many professionals advise that older accounts should neither be closed nor canceled, as it is likely to affect your credit score.

There's a high possibility of you having a high credit score by having a long time with your credit.

The Number of Credit Applications

Lastly, the number of applications to your credit slightly affects your credit score. Every time you apply for a loan or possibly a credit card (even if not yet approved), your credit score slightly decreases.

Opening various credit accounts within a very short time can be very risky for financial institutions, especially when it's a case of one who does not have a lengthy credit history. This explains why many people see that their credit score has decreased either when they open a credit card or when they are approved for a particular loan. However, the decline is temporary.

Also, bear in mind that credit checks vary. Interestingly, checking your credit will have your credit score reduced if and only if it is a hard inquiry. There are hard inquiries and soft inquiries, which I will explain below.

The hard inquiry is made when a loan is applied with a lender. That may include a student loan, car, mortgage loan. These inquiries affect your credit score.

While the soft inquiry is made when you request a copy of your credit report, apply for a job or use it for a credit monitoring service. These types of inquiries in no way affect your credit score.

How Exactly Is It Calculated?

As important as it is to calculate your credit score, it is also very important to know that these factors have no fixed percentage. They may vary due to the financial information obtained from your credit report.

This goes to say that without adequate knowledge of the basic factors above, there is a tendency for an individual to be careless in the decisions he makes at obtaining a high credit score. It is hence very important that these factors are known.

Though these factors are applied when calculating a credit report, the level of importance varies from person to person.

It is not possible to record the impact of each factor on the credit score without acknowledging the report as a whole.

How to Check Your Credit Score

Some services enable you to check your credit score at very little or no cost. However, you must take caution and use services that you know are reliable so that you don't fall into the hands of scammers on the Internet. Some of these reliable services, especially those listed below, have no cost.

Chapter 3. May I Achieve a Score Of "800+"?

Have Savings

Now it is time for the hard part. Maybe you have been doing some of the work that we go through in this guidebook, and you have seen a nice increase in the amount of your FICO score.

This is always good news, but now we want to see if we can get our score to 800 or higher. Only the elite have this kind of score. It is hard to get it because it requires a perfect balance of credit types, a high credit limit, and no missed payments, among other things. But it is possible.

When you can get your credit to be this high, it is a lot easier for you to go through and get credit and loans at any time you would like. If something happens and you have many medical bills to deal with, this credit score can help you take care of it. It can also be used for non-emergencies like if you would like to start a business, get a new house, or do something else along the same lines.

How do you make sure that you can get your credit score up to 800 or higher? The first thing is to know the facts. Once you can answer the main question of "What is a perfect credit score?" you will find that it is easier to take on the right steps to figure out exactly what you can do to reach the perfect score. First, though, you need to make sure you know where you stand on the FICO scale.

Once a year, you can get a free annual credit report from any of the country's top credit bureaus, all three of them. If you go through this and find any issues on any of them (sometimes a mistake will show up on one and not on the others), this is the time to fix them. You will never get to an 800+ score if there are many errors in your report.

The next thing you can focus on is establishing a long history of credit.

With a few exceptions, lenders will most of the time view borrowers with short histories of credit as riskier to work with. To reach a credit score that is 800 or higher, you have to establish and then also maintain a long history. Even if you are not using some of the accounts, keeping them open will help you get that score up.

As we have mentioned a bit before, you need to make sure that all of your bills are paid on time. There isn't a single person who has an 800+ credit score who also has a missed payment, or a bunch of missed payments, on their report. Paying your bills late or not paying the bills at all is going to decrease your score. If you have trouble remembering the due dates, then consider signing up so for automatic payments and have that taken care of for you.

You also need to take the time to redefine your credit card usage. About 30 percent of the score you have will consist of the utilization rate for your credit, which will be the amount of debt you owe divided by the total credit available. Typically, we want to stay under 30 percent, but if you are trying to get a higher score, then staying under 10 percent is best.

What we haven't talked about much in this guide, but will help you get that higher score you want, is to learn how to diversify the accounts you are holding onto. This is one of the best ways to strengthen your credit, and while it can take some time to accomplish this, you will find it is a great way for us to make sure your credit score can go up.

You can make your credit score stronger when you can diversify your accounts. This is not an excuse to go out there and open up 10 different card accounts at a time. It means that you should have a mix of different types of credit, such as an auto loan, a student loan, a mortgage, and a credit card. Ten credit cards will not be a diverse mix of debt or show responsibility with your score. But having a bunch of different accounts, even if some of them have been paid off, will be a much better option to work with.

While you work on your credit score, you need to make sure that you cut your spending and create a budget that you can stick with.

This helps you stay within means that you can afford and makes it less likely that you will fall into trouble with your spending. Although, indeed, your credit is not going to factor in your income, living within your means, no matter what that number is, is a great way to raise your score.

Next on the list is to find ways to limit the liability you are dealing with. When you co-sign a loan, remember that this may seem like a nice thing to do, but you are taking on a risk for another person. If you do this for someone who cannot manage their debt all that well, it will negatively affect your score because you will be responsible for that debt as well. If you want to make sure that you can get a credit score that is 800+ and maintain that, then it is a good idea to avoid cosigning at all.

In addition to this, you should make sure that your liability is limited in other manners as well. You should always report cards that have been lost or stolen right away. If you don't do this, then it is likely that you will be liable for any of the purchases that are not authorized at the time. And if you are not able to afford those purchases, then your score is going to be the thing that suffers here.

And finally, you need to make sure that you are restricting the hard inquiries that happen to your report. Whether you or another agency or institution is pulling out the credit report and asking for a copy of it, you are dealing with an inquiry. A soft inquiry can happen on occasion, and it is generally not going to be enough to make any changes to your credit. This soft inquiry is going to happen when one of the following occurs:

- You go through and do a check on your credit report.

- You give an employer you may work with in the future permission to go through and check your credit.

- You have the financial institutions that you do business with go through and check your credit.

- You get a credit card offer that has been preapproved, and that specific company goes through and checks your credit.

While the soft inquiry is not going to do all that much to your credit scores, you need to be careful about the hard inquiry. This is going to be the one that can affect your credit score. This is when a company pulls up your credit report after applying for a product like a credit card or a mortgage. You want to make sure that you can limit the hard inquiries as much as possible to get the best results with this.

Chapter 4. The Right Way to Check Your Credit Report

The business uses the credit and pays the bill promptly. As the business has established a positive business credit profile and continues using the credit and paying the bills on time, it will qualify for more credit.

The first step in business credit building is for the business owner to order a business credit report. The business owner needs to know what is being reported for that business regarding both positive and derogatory information. The business owner will also want to actively monitor the business credit building and score building as it is taking place.

Business Credit Reports

When they receive their Business Information Report from D&B, many business owners find that they have a low PAYDEX score. They scratch their heads and wonder why their score is low even when paying the bills on time.

Other information on this report includes the total dollar amount of all trades reported, the largest amount that anyone trade has reported, and the percentage of payments that have been made to the top ten (10) industries.

Once a business sets up its credit report and pays some bills on time, it should have a high PAYDEX score. It is then vital that the business maintains its report.

The business owner should check the business report periodically. They may want to consider purchasing the Monitoring Service that D&B offers. This service allows a business to receive alerts when new positive or negative information appears on the report. There are several areas that a business owner will be notified of if they change, including:

- Credit Rating

- Suits, liens or business judgments

- PAYDEX score changes

- Changes to financial statements

- Other significant business news

The business credit file must remain accurate. The Fair Credit Reporting Act does not apply to businesses as it does with consumer reports. If there is something wrong in the business credit report, or if a step is skipped in setting it up, there is no legal recourse to have that information removed. If the file was set up incorrectly, there's a good chance the business credit file could be put in the "High Risk" category, making it nearly impossible to remove inaccuracies.

This is your Credit Scorecard as of 05/20/2016. Come back after 30 days to refresh it.

740	28	2 years	21	1%	0
FICO SCORE	Total Accounts	Length of Credit	Inquiries	Revolving Utilization	Missed Payments

Your FICO® Score based on Experian data

740

FICO® Scores range from 300 - 850

How lenders see your score

Very Good

FICO® Scores in the range of 740 - 799 are considered very good

Your FICO® Score compared to the U.S. average by age

See what's affecting your FICO® Score

↑ What's helping   ↓ What's hurting

Now that we have taken some time to look at the different things that are going to raise your credit score, we also need to take a closer look at some of the different parts that will end up harming the credit scores that we have. If you are in the process of fixing your credit, you want to make sure that you are careful and that you are not going to end up doing something that will harm your credit in the process. Some of the different things that we can watch out for when it comes to harming your credit score include:

What's Harming My Credit Score

Paying Late or Not at All

One of the worst things that you can do when it comes to your credit score is paying late on anything. About 35 percent of your score will be about your history of making payments or not on time. Consistently being late on these payments will cause a lot of damage to your credit score. Always pay your bills on time, especially your credit card bills.

What is even worse than paying late is not paying at all. If you decide to completely ignore your cards and other bills and not pay them at all, then you are going to be in even more trouble as well. Each month that you miss out on a payment for your credit card, you are going to end up one month closer to helping your account be charged off.

If you ever want a chance to get your credit score up at all, especially if you are hoping to get it up to 800 or higher, then you have to stop the late payments. This will be a bad thing because it shows that you are not willing to pay your money back, and they are less likely to give you some more money in the process.

For those struggling with making payments, whether these payments are often late or they don't come in at all, it is time to get a budget in place. You live above your means, which is never a good sign of getting your score up to where you would like. When you can get your budget in place and start paying your debts on time, you will be able to get that credit score higher in no time.

Having an Account Charged Off or Sent to Collections

Next on the list is having your accounts charged off. When creditors are worried that you will never pay your bills for loans or credit cards, they will use a process known as charging off your accounts. A charge off means that the insurer has pretty much given up on ever hearing from you again. This does not mean that you are no longer going to hold responsibility for this debt at all. This is one of the absolute worst things out there regarding your credit score.

Another issue is when one of your accounts is sent off to collections. Creditors are often going to work with debt collectors to collect a payment out of you. Collectors could send your account to collections after, but sometimes before, charging it all off. This is never a good thing, even if the account is charged off at that time, either.

If you are to the point of your bills going to collections or being charged off, this means that you have not just missed one or two payments. It means that you have gone so long without paying the whole thing that the company figures they will never get it back. Either they have probably written it off as a tax break or they have sold it to a credit collection company that will be bothering you a lot in the future.

This is never a good thing. You will be harassed for a long time to come about all of that. It will show other creditors that you have not just missed a few payments when things get tough. It shows them that you fell so far behind that someone else, someone who had given you money in the past, decided to give up on you in the process. This is hard to fight against and will not make a new creditor feel like they should loan you the needed money.

Filing Bankruptcy

This is a bit extreme that you should avoid at all costs. Bankruptcy is an extreme measure, and it will cause a lot of devastation to the score you are working with. It will also be on your record for seven to ten years. It is a good idea to seek alternatives, like working with counselors for consumer credit, before filing bankruptcy.

It is best if you can do everything that you can to avoid bankruptcy at all costs. It may seem like the best idea to work with. You assume that you can just walk away from all of the debt that you have and not have to worry about it ever again when you declare bankruptcy. This is not really how this whole process will work for you at all, though.

There are several types of bankruptcies that you can work with, but you will often need to go through and pay off as much of the debts as possible. And sometimes, this can be several years of making payments and having your wages garnished and taken away before you can even get to bankruptcy. You could just pay the debts for that amount of time instead, or make some kind of agreement with the creditors for a lower amount if needed, and now have the black mark of the bankruptcy on your side.

Once the bankruptcy is complete, which can take some time, a new problem will occur. You have to focus on how you will handle the black mark on your credit report for quite a bit of time. This could be anywhere from seven to ten years. And you can bet that creditors are not going to look all that kindly at that. You will find that it is almost impossible to get any kind of credit or any other monetary help you need for a long time afterward.

If you cannot get on a budget and take control over your debts, you may get it all discharged, but then you are going to turn around, and before you know it, all of your money is gone again, and you are facing bankruptcy again. This is never a good thing. You will not be offered the option of bankruptcy multiple times, and using this as a Band-Aid is not going to work.

To avoid bankruptcy, you need to learn how to work with a budget and figure out the best ways to manage your money, no matter what the income is that you are working with. This is easier to manage than you may think and can help you get on a good payment schedule so that you can deal with your debts and get them paid off. Bankruptcy seems like an easy way to get out of debt. Still, it haunts you for many years afterward. It can make getting credit later on almost impossible, and it will not solve the underlying problem that got you to this situation.

High Balances or Maxed Out Cards

We always need to take a look at the balances that we are going to have on our credit cards all of the time. The second most important part that comes with our credit score is the amount of debt on them, which will be measured out by credit utilization. Having high balances for credit cards, relative to the credit limit you are working with, will increase credit utilization and make your credit score go down. For example, if you have a limit of $10,000 on a card, but the balance is $9500 or higher, your score will not positively reflect this one.

We also need to make sure that we are not maxing out or going over the limit regarding our credit cards. Credit cards that are over the limit or maxed out will make the credit utilization that you have at 100 percent. This will be one of the most damaging things that you can do with your credit score. Make sure to pay down those debts as fast as possible to maintain your credit score and keep it from going over the top.

Closing Credit Cards

There are a few ways that closing your card will end up with a decrease in your credit score. First, we need to look at closing up a card that still has a balance. When you close that card, the credit limit you get to work with will end up at $0, while your balance is still going to be the same. This will make it look like you have been able to max out the credit card, which will cause your score to drop a bit. If you want to close your account, you need to make sure that you pay off the balance before closing it.

Another thing to consider is what will happen when you close out your old credit cards. About 15 percent of your credit score will be the length of your credit history, and longer credit histories will be better. Closing up old cards, especially some of the oldest cards, are going to make your history seem like it is a lot shorter than it is. Even if you do not use the card anymore, and there are no annual fees, you should keep the card open because you are losing nothing and gaining more.

And finally, we need to be careful about closing cards with available credit. If you have more than one credit card to work with, some that have balanced and some without these, then closing the cards that do not have a balance will increase the credit utilization. You can just keep those all out of the way and see your credit report go up.

Not Having Enough Mix on the Report

While this is not as big of a deal as some of the other options, you will find that having a good mix of credit will be about 10 percent of your credit score at the time. If you have a report that only has one or two things on it, such as either credit cards or loans, the score you are working with will likely be affected somehow.

The more you can mix up your accounts and get them to have many different things on them, the better. You don't want to overextend yourself, but having a mix of loans, mortgage, credit cards, and more that you pay off each month without fail is going to be one of the best ways that you can raise your credit score without causing harm or paying too much in the process.

This does not mean that you should go out and apply for many different things all at once to get your mix up. This often happens; naturally, the longer you work on your credit score. You may have a few credit cards, and then you take out a loan for a car and pay it off. Maybe you need a loan for a vacation or some home improvement, so you will have those accounts and then get a mortgage.

As time goes on, these different loans and credit amounts will come and go, but they will all show up in the credit mix and help increase your score. If you try and increase your mix all at once, you will bring up some red flags against your credit, which can cause some issues. Doing this over a few years as you need it is the best way to make sure that your credit score goes up.

Applying for Too Much

Another thing that will count on your report is the credit inquiries. These will take up about 10 percent of the score you work with. Making several applications for loans and credit in a short amount of time will cause a big drop in your credit score along the way. Always keep the applications for credit to a minimum, so this doesn't end up harming you along the way.

In some cases, this is not going to harm you too much. For example, if you have a good credit score and you want to apply for a mortgage, you will want to apply for a few mortgages and shop around a bit. If you do these close together, it will not be seen as bad because the lender will assume this is what you are doing, rather than you taking on too much or that you have been turned down. You can also explain this to them easily if they ask.

For most other cases, though, this will not be a good sign. Having all of those inquiries on your score will slightly lower it, at least for the short term. And when other lenders see that you are applying for a lot of credit, they will assume that you are getting rejected. They will wonder why or they will assume that you are taking on too much credit that you will not handle, and they will not want to lend you any money either.

These are just a few of the different things that we are going to work with when the time comes to handle our credit report. Sometimes the things that can harm your score will be much more important than the things that can help improve the score. Working on both is going to be important when it all comes down to it as well, and knowing how to avoid some of the common things that can ruin your credit in no time is imperative to getting that score up and seeing it work the way that you want.

Chapter 5. How to Repair Your Negative Profile

Fixing your credit is possible and not as difficult as you have been made to believe. No matter how bad your credit score seems, the ways to magically boost it are, in fact, simple and practical. Contrary to common myths that a credit score may become so poor that it cannot be fixed, no credit score can be fixed. Whenever you find the need to fix one, apply the following strategies:

Identify Theft Claim

Over 16 million Americans are victims of identity theft. This is a large population, so anyone could be a victim. Identity theft is a crime, which involves the police, so ensure you are ready to go this route. If you are sure that your score has been ruined because of identity theft, you can use this method. Abusing this method could land you into trouble with the law. Here is how to dispute using the method:

- Step 1: Report the matter to the police, then get a copy of your report from the local sheriff (you will need this report later)

- Step 2: File the dispute with FTC

- Step 3: Go on to dispute with various credit bureaus.

- Step 4: Set up an identity theft alert (be sure to know what this means in terms of your access to credit)

Pay the Original Creditor

When your debt is sold to collection agencies, you will probably risk having new items showing up on your credit report, which can further hurt your credit rating. However, you can stop by sending a check with the full payment of any outstanding amount to the original creditor.

You just send proof of payment to that collection agency and any other, then request them to delete any derogatory items they have reported from your credit report.

It is always a good idea to be in direct contact with your creditor or creditors. Many of these agencies will be fully equipped to cheat you and follow through on plans to have your report show bad credit scores.

It is up to you to remove these "middlemen" and do the payment yourself. You could also agree to pay a portion of the money to the creditor as full payment for the sum (the pay-to-delete strategy).

Under federal law, if the original creditor accepts any payment as full payment for any outstanding debt, the collection agency must remove whatever they have reported. This will only work if the original creditor accepts the payment; it is possible for some of the checks you pay to the original creditor to be returned to you.

Pay to Delete

If you have derogatory items in your credit report, you can opt to pay the unpaid credit balance only if the creditor agrees to delete the items from your credit report. As I already mentioned, don't agree with a $0 balance appearing on your credit report since this taints your reputation. As a rule of thumb, less is more in this section; the fewer items you have here, the better off for you. This method works through the idea that your report doesn't show whether you have had any history of bad credit in the derogatory items section. This will ultimately improve your rating. The idea is to ensure that whatever amount you agree to pay doesn't show up as your last activity date. If the creditor only cares about their money, why should they bother telling the world you have finally paid?

In most instances, the creditors often write off debts within just 2 years of constantly defaulting. This information is sold in bulk to a collection company for some pennies or a dollar. This means that the collection companies will be just fine if you even pay a fraction of what you ought to pay. Whatever you pay, they will still make money! This makes them open to negotiations such as pay-to-delete since they have nothing to lose anyway.

Therefore, only use the pay-to-delete approach at this level and not any other. The only other way around it for the collection company is a judgment, which can be costly, so you have some advantage.

Additionally, you can use this strategy when new negative items start showing up in your report that could hurt your reputation as a credit consumer.

Also, since the creditors will often sell the same information to multiple collection companies, you might probably start noting the same debt reported by several companies; use pay-to-delete to get them off your report.

You can also use this strategy if you have not successfully got items off your credit report using other methods. Opting to go the dispute way might only make the process cyclic, cumbersome, tiresome, and frustrating; you don't want to get into this cycle.

Now that you know when to use this method, understanding how the entire process works is critical. To start with, ensure that you get an acceptance in writing if they agree to your terms; don't pay without the letter! After you agree, allow about 45 days for the next credit report to be availed to you by your credit monitoring service. These companies have the legal power to initiate the deletion process, so don't accept anything less such as updating the balance; it is either a deletion or nothing. If they try to stall the process by saying that they cannot delete, mention that it will only take about 5 minutes to fill the Universal Data Form. Don't worry if one company doesn't seem to agree with your terms, another one will probably show up and gladly take the offer.

In any case, what do they have to gain when they keep your debt when you are willing to pay? Remember that the records will only be kept for 7 years, so these companies have no other choice if 2 years have already passed. However, don't use this as an excuse for not paying your debts, since the creditors can sue you to compel you to pay outstanding amounts.

This process aims to ensure that whatever bad experience you have with one creditor doesn't make the others make unfavorable decisions on your part.

Note: don't be overly aggressive with creditors who have a lot to lose in the process, especially recent creditors, since they can probably sue you. Your goal is only to be aggressive with creditors barred by the statute of limitations from suing you in court. You don't want to find yourself in legal trouble to add to your existing problems. Try and remain as smart as possible and make all the right moves to help you repair your credit at the earliest.

Pay-to-delete isn't the only option available to you; you can use other strategies to repair your credit.

Settle Your Debt

Total debt owed accounts for up to 30% of the credit score, so don't overlook this. This includes personal loans, car loans, and credit utilization. You should also calculate the credit utilization ratio (the balance you carry in your revolving fund compared to your credit).

As your credit utilization increases, your credit score goes down; aim to keep your credit card balances no more than 30% of your credit card limit. You should even aim for zero balances since this means a higher credit score. Combine this strategy with the pay-to-delete strategy.

To pay your debts, you can use snowballing or avalanching strategies. Snowballing involves paying off debts with the lowest balance first, then closing them as you move up to the bigger debts.

Avalanching involves paying debts starting from those with the highest interest rates as you move down.

Look Out for Errors in the Report

93% of the credit reports have been proven to have errors. Look out for any of these, then file a dispute. Such things as the last date of activity, write-off date, wrong account name or number, and others could be enough to taint your credit. Don't overlook any of that. If the report has an error, don't be discouraged by the credit bureau's stalling tactics; mention the Notice (Summons) and complaint to make them know that you know what the law requires of them. The bureaus wouldn't want to have their systems investigated and proven to be weak/flawed, so this strategy can compel them to correct errors and thus boosting your credit.

Your credit report should be free of errors. Even the slightest thing as reporting the wrong date of last activity on your credit report is enough to damage your credit. Your last date of activity has a profound effect on your credit rating. If the write-off date is different from what has been reported, you can dispute the entry to have it corrected to reflect your credit's actual status. However, keep in mind that the credit bureaus will, in most instances, confirm that the negative entry is correct even if this is not the case, which means that they will not remove the erroneous item.

You must put in efforts to get them on the right track. To get them to comply, you must inform them that the law requires them to have a preponderance of their systems to ensure that these errors do not arise. Therefore, the mere fact of confirming the initial error is not enough. Inform them about the notice (summons) and complaint to understand that you are serious about the matter. Once they have an idea of your stance, they will put in efforts to do the right thing. The bureaus don't want any case to go to court since this could ultimately prove that their systems are weak or flawed, which means they will probably be in big trouble. So, try and drive a strong point across so that they understand you mean business. The mere exchange of emails will not do, and you must send them details on how strong your case will be. This will make them understand their position and decide to help you avoid going to court. This will, in turn, work to your advantage in making them dig deeper into the issue. However, this method will only work if you are certain that an error was made. You will also require proof for it and cannot simply state an error.

Mix-Spread Your Credit

This usually affects your credit score by up to 10%. Having more credit signifies that you can handle your finances properly, making you creditworthy, especially if you have a good payment history.

Request for Proof of the Original Debt

Suppose you are certain that the credit card has been written off for late payment. In that case, the carriers (Capital One and

Citibank) likely cannot find the original billing statements within 30 days, which they are required by the law to respond. This, in effect, allows you to have whatever entry you have disputed removed from the credit report as if it never happened.

Another handy approach is requesting the original contract that you signed to be provided. This is to prove that you opened that particular credit card in the first instance. As you do this, don't just ask for "verification" since this just prompts the collection agency to "verify" that they received a request for collection on an account that has your name on it. Therefore, as a rule of thumb, ensure that you state clearly that you want them to provide proof of the debt, including providing billing statements for the last several months and the original contract that you signed when opening the credit card account.

Handy Tips to Improve Your Score

Settle Your Bills Promptly

Payment history accounts for 35% of your credit score, making it one of the score's biggest determinants. This is pretty straightforward; when you pay your bills on time, your score will improve. You could even set up automatic payments to ensure that you won't miss payments since the amounts are deducted from your account. The biggest contributors to this include collections, bankruptcies, and different late payments. You should note that the recent delinquencies have a greater effect than the old ones; 70% of the score is determined by whatever has happened within the past 2 years.

Watch Out for Fair Debt Collection Practices Act "FDCPA" Violations

The law is very clear on what collection agencies can do and what they cannot do as far as debt collection is concerned. For instance:

1. They should not call you more than once a day unless they can prove that their automated systems accidentally dialed it.

2. They cannot call you before 8:00 a.m. or after 9:00 p.m.

3. They cannot threaten, belittle, or yell at you to make you pay any outstanding debts.

4. They cannot tell anyone else other than your spouse why they are contacting you.

5. The best way to go about this is to let them know that you record all their calls.

6. They cannot take more money from your account than you have authorized if they do an ACH.

7. They are also not allowed to send you collection letters if you have already sent them a cease and desist order.

If you can prove that collection companies violate the laws, you should file a complaint with the company then have your lawyer send proof indicating the violations; you can then request that any outstanding debt be forgiven. You need to understand that the law is on your side in such circumstances. If the violations are major, the collection companies could be forced to pay fines of up to $10,000 for these violations.

So, if your debt is significantly lower than this, you could be on your way to having your debt cleared since these companies would rather pay your debt than pay the fine. Every violation of the Fair Debt Collection Practices Act is punishable by a fine of up to $1000, which is payable to you, so don't just think of this as something that cannot amount to anything repairing your credit is concerned.

Chapter 6. How to Convert Bad Credit into Good Credit

How to Bust Common Credit Myths

Loans have become a great tool that helps people solve their financial issues in no time. Although, beyond the several advantages and responsibilities, there are certain myths that we must be aware of and break. If you have plans to acquire a loan but are not sure if it's your best option, this book will show you how to see and handle the situation exactly as you should.

While some of us like credit score as it has favored us in our ability to handle it well, others see it as one that does more harm than good, which is not the case. The issue with people who do not enjoy the credit score is because they were misinformed on some things and it leads them to fall into traps they could have avoided if they had the right information all along. That's why in this section of this book, we will be discussing the eight common myths to break on credit score. These myths are:

When You Close Your Many Credit Accounts, Your Credit Score Will Improve

This may seem logically sound but is completely false. The way credit scores are calculated in parts is known as the credit/ debt ratio. The agencies who calculate your score evaluate the amount of debt you have and the amount of credit available for you to draw.

So let's assume you have ten credit cards and the credit availability all sums up to $100,000 and you have used only $15,000 of that available credit, your credit utilization rate becomes 15%. This is known as positive since you have 85% of your unused credit.

Let's take the case of you closing seven accounts because you're not using them. You will still have $15,000 in debt, but in this case, your total credit now available drops to $30,000. This means that your credit utilization rate has skyrocketed by 50%, hence your credit score dropping.

Do not close credit cards like this. It is better to put the cards away safely. And if there's a chance you can increase your credit limit, go for it. As long as you are not maximizing it, it will help your credit score.

Once You Have a Bad Credit Score, It Is Impossible to Get Loans or Credits

This myth has been derived from advertisements that require a good credit score to get funding. Interestingly, almost everyone can get funding no matter what their credit score may be, whether it is increased in the 800s or lower in the 400s.

What a credit score represents to financial institutions is a level of risk as this determines, to a large extent, the terms of any loan or credit received. Let's say, for example, someone who has a credit score of 800, the individual will be considered low risk for the financial institution. They already know that this person pays in good time, has available credit in high quantity and has longevity with his accounts. This will hence result in a low-interest rate and more credit available.

However, someone with a credit score of 450 will be considered high-risk. The reason is that the loans and credits will be available but will have oppressive interest rates for very few credits.

Credit Scores Tend to Change Only a Few Times a Year

Credit scores are usually in constant change. The information with which you calculate your score is derived from the financial institutions you maintain business relationships with. If you miss making a payment, it will reflect almost immediately. If you go ahead to close multiple accounts, the information will have an impact on your score much earlier than 3 or 6 months.

Looking at your credit score now, you can be able to see the latest updates that have been made. The time actually varies as sometimes it can be a matter of hours, days or even weeks. Knowing this, you should ensure to check your credit score on a regular basis. So in case something bad happens, you can address it early enough.

One Thing That Affects Your Score Is the Amount of Money You Make

This is so not true. Your credit score does not list the employers' income but rather the credit accounts. So regardless of what you earn a year, whether you're a CEO who earns 3 million a year or an entry-level worker who earns $30,000 a year, your income does not determine your credit score. Interestingly, even with so much money, a wealthy CEO might have a bad credit score because of bankruptcy or successions of late payments in the previous years.

The only way that your income can affect your credit score is if you live a Champagne lifestyle and having only a beer budget. That can be financially unhealthy for you. If it happens that you run out of your cards, by making minimum payments and losing them completely, your score gradually becomes a great success, as it should.

Bringing a Balance to Your Credit Card Also Helps Your Score

No, not at all. To be quite frank, it doesn't hurt that either. But you would be wrong to think that keeping money on your card helps your score because it really doesn't. Ideally, I advise you to pay the balances on your cards fully every month in order to avoid paying interest on purchases. If you're just paying the minimum, then you're not doing yourself any good and wasting your money. Most of this minimum payment can be paid to the credit card company, as only a small fraction pays the balance.

Do not bring a balance whenever possible. And if your balance exceeds 30% of your card, you should consider transferring from half to another card. When one-third of the credit is used on a card, then that can actually damage the credit score. In an ideal case, the balance ought to be less than 30% of the credit available; the lower it is, the better for you. This will be a good place to request a credit line increase, so as your line is increased by a few thousand dollars, your balance is affected and falls below 30%, hence increasing your credit score.

You Can Have an Excellent Credit Report If You Have No Credit

The lack of credit is a good thing in some countries, but not in the US. If you have never had a credit card or a car loan, you must be financially responsible. But as for the United States, your credit history determines your credit score. Good credit history equals a good credit score and vice versa.

All in all, credit scores are built. Financial institutions who lend loans and credits want to know that you will borrow money and pay it back on time coupled with interest. Once they see that, then you are safe from any risk.

You Can't Recover from a Bad Credit Score. It Stays with You for Life

If you currently have a poor credit score, it is not the end of the world. If you are paying exorbitant interest rates now, you won't be doing so forever. Although repairing and rebuilding take time and patience.

CATEGORY	SCORE
Excellent (30% of People)	750 - 850
Good (13% of People)	700 - 749
Fair (18% of People)	650 - 699
Poor (34% of People)	550 - 649
BAD (16% of People)	350 - 549

Stick with the basics and be consistent with it. Open new credit lines and pay your credit card bills in time. Try never to miss a payment. Make your balances low at all times. Keep a very steady but low credit usage ratio. Do not apply to many cards or accounts in a year.

Once you can do these, your credit score will change for the better, even amidst all financial difficulties.

Chapter 7. Quickest and Easiest Strategies to Raise Your Score

Pay Off What You Owe

While this is going to be easier said than done in most situations, according to Experian, the ideal amount of credit utilization that you want is 30 percent or less. While there are other ways to increase your credit utilization rating, paying off what you owe on time each month will also go towards showing you can pay your bills on time, essentially pulling double duty when it comes to improving your credit score. It will also make it easier to follow through on the following tips.

Pay the Bills the Day You Get Them

This might take some discipline, but it's a great system to stay on track - pay your bills on the same day they arrive in the mail. If you have online banking, this will be quite easy: the bill arrives, you go to your computer or smartphone and log into your bank account, and you pay your bill. Done. One less thing on your mind and zero risk of being late with the payment.

Very often we are lulled into a false reality by bill due dates that are weeks away. You look at your account and think: I have a thousand bucks in there. Meanwhile, you have three bills laying around for half of that amount. Your discretionary spending (wants, not needs) is quite different when you think you have X amount in your account rather than X minus bills. By paying your bills right away, you get them out of the way and won't forget to pay them. You are also going to spend less money because your account will be a more honest reflection of your financial picture.

It is incredible how easy it is to get into trouble financially when everything is payable in a month. We lose touch with where we really stand in terms of money. If you cannot afford to pay every bill as it comes in, maybe take out a small loan to bring you to square one, and then chip away at the loan.

Get A Cash Secured Loan

Similar to the secured credit card, you can build and repair credit by taking out a cash-secured loan. In this case, offer the bank to borrow x amount and use that amount as collateral on the loan. The funds will be locked down in a savings account and you will gain access to the borrowed funds once the loan is paid in full.

The advantage to the bank is that they have zero risk (they repay the loan with the savings if the deal goes south), they make a profit on the deal since the rate they pay on savings deposit is lower than the rate you pay on the loan, and the loan officer is happy about getting another sale.

A good idea is to borrow an amount like $5,000 to $10,000 and repay it over the next 3 to 5 years with regular scheduled payments. As long as there are no late payments, this will count as a positive on your credit history. Do not repay the loan immediately, as you want the loan to run for a long time for maximum effect.

If the loan is repaid within a few months, it might not even have a chance of making a good impact on your credit score. As a bonus, once the loan is paid off, you will have access to the savings. This is often done by some creative lenders to help young people build credit and can be a forced savings plan for a future home purchase down payment.

Negotiate to Repay Written Off Items

Sometimes our mistakes are in the past, and we are still paying for them in the present. Unpaid collections and written-off loans and credit card balances not only look horrible on your credit history but also greatly reduce your credit score.

A write-off is basically when the lender decides that they have no chance of recovering the amount owed to them by you. They write off the amount on their books and inform the credit bureaus. If you are able to do so, you should seriously consider paying any written-off debts that you may have. You can often do so on favorable terms.

Call up the company that wrote off the debt and inform them that you would like to make amends by paying back some or all of the debt you owed them and that was written off. This will basically be free money for them, as they have already made provisions for the loss. It makes the manager look good. Your condition should be that once the written-off debt has been repaid by you, they will have to report to the credit bureaus and inform them of the change. Get this in writing and forward a copy of the letter to the credit bureaus. This will erase the negative entry on your credit history and make your credit score shoot upwards.

If you are brave, you can also try to negotiate the amount it will take to remove the write-off. Ask them to reverse any fees that might have been added over the course of the debt being delinquent. Sometimes they will also remove accrued interest from the debt and aim to recover only the initial amount owed to them less any payments made. You can also just bluff and say you only have x amount and are willing to pay that to them in return for the credit history adjustment. Sometimes, they will think that 40% recovered is better than 0% and go for it.

The point of all of this is that these things are not permanent and can be fixed if you are willing to make the effort.

When Rate Shopping, Do It Quickly

Every time there is an inquiry on your credit history, your score drops by about 10 points. If you are buying a new car or applying for a mortgage, you are likely to approach a few different lenders in order to get the best rate. Often their pricing is dependent on your credit score, and they will need to view your credit history first before providing a quote.

When you apply at just one bank, one inquiry is fine and won't affect your credit score much. However, it gets complicated when there are five or six different banks taking a look over a long period of time (one every weekend, for instance). The credit bureaus understand that you might have to go through this process to get the best rate possible, they will not penalize you for multiple inquiries within a short period of time.

There is no specific time period to rate shop, but generally, you don't want to be looking around for more than a week. Two weeks at the most if you want to take a risk.

Keeping all credit inquiries within a short time period is a little easier done for mortgages since a house purchase is usually a very planned out process, and you can therefore stack a few mortgage appointments in one week. It is much harder when buying a car and applying for car loans to keep within a short time period. You might get pre-approved at your local bank, but then get roped into financing through the dealership when you finally find the right car a few weeks later. The local bank will pull a credit history and the dealership will send the loan application out to multiple lenders, who will all likely look at the credit history again.

In order to avoid taking multiple hits to your credit score, try to wrap up your rate and loan shopping in a short period of time. There are also many banks out there that do not price your rate based on your credit score - these banks will be able to quote you a rate without pulling your credit history first. Once you officially apply for the loan, they will review the credit history for underwriting.

Avoid Over-Extending Yourself

People who live within their means usually have great credit. People who want to buy everything, and borrow every penny possible, usually have lousy credit. If you borrow too much, you will eventually run into problems making the payments. You can have a lot of debt and decent credit at the same time, but someday something might happen and cause the whole house of cards to fall down.

Often it takes a long time until problems become really obvious. Many people who have overextended themselves will keep things afloat for a while, usually by borrowing more and more. First, they will forgo saving for retirement, then maintaining the house, then suddenly there is only enough to make the bare minimum payments on the credit cards and soon new debt is taken out to pay for the old debt.

Banks will bail you out as often as they can because your banker is only a human and does not want to push you off the cliff. They will bail you out by giving more credit and then some more until the day comes when there is no more room left. When that moment comes, the wall goes up and you are alone. Soon payments start coming in late and your credit score takes a nosedive. Once your credit history takes a hit, the chance of getting bailed out becomes even smaller.

For excessive debt to cause a drop in your credit score, you don't even need to be late on your payments. The amount you have borrowed and the level of use of revolving credit, such as credit cards and lines of credit, can cause a drop in your score. At some point, the credit bureau computer notices that large credit card balances are not actually going down month to month. It may decide that you are over your means and reward you with a lower score to scare off lenders.

Set rules for yourself and your family when it comes to borrowing. You can't really avoid a mortgage, but things like car purchases and vacations should have rules. When buying a car, try to buy everything in cash. If that is not possible, aim to have at least a 15% down payment on the purchase price. If you can't even come up with that, maybe you need to wait or buy a cheaper car. Boats, snowmobiles, motorcycles: these are toys and you really should not borrow 100% of the purchase price to buy them. The same goes for vacations: don't borrow money to go on vacation. If you already did, don't borrow for the next vacation before you have paid off the previous one.

These borrowing rules suck and they are no fun, but they will put you on a much better financial footing and help you avoid the kind of overspending that will lead to credit problems.

Learn to Budget

Budgeting is a pain in the rear, even for people who are doing great financially. It is boring and it is restrictive, it sucks the lifeblood right out of you. Reaching or exceeding your monthly allowance for restaurant meals in a week is not fun. And where do unexpected dentist expenses go? What about roof repairs?

In many years as a lender for a bank, I have given out hundreds of booklets on budgeting and personally given advice on the subject. There is a psychological barrier that makes budgets so difficult. Everyone thinks they need to be perfect and on a budget all the time, and once you go over your budget in even the least important category, you feel like you broke your perfect record.

Once perfection has been tainted, the baby is thrown out with the bathwater and the habit of budgeting is abandoned. Maybe abandoning your budget reinforces your belief that budgets are hard and you are bad with money. You need to get past this and do your best to stick with it.

Budgets are like Bootcamps for fat kids. There is that sick feeling at first when your body is woken up to reality. Then there are all the steps that follow that you just keep messing up on and never really getting perfect. Then there is the cheating every once in a while when you somehow manage to get your hands on a bag of chips. After it's all said and done, it was no fun, you didn't do everything perfectly, but you still walked away a little better or even much better than before.

The point of a budget is to put everything down on paper. How much money is coming in every month? How much money is going out? Is less money going out than coming in, but you are still going further into debt? Then you either missed a few items or are not totally honest with yourself, you will need to start again. Just knowing how razor-thin the margin is between how much is coming in and how much is going out might stop you from buying that cookbook that you will never use. Sit down and do your budget and be brutally honest. You don't even need to try to save money consciously, you subconsciously start spending less.

Break your spending into different categories and decide how much you should spend on each category. Figure out the costs you cannot change, such as rent or mortgage payments or car insurance. Then figure out what your discretionary spending is, these are the things that are wants and not needs. Those are the categories that you can save money on. Set a budget and try to hit it. Celebrate every time you decide not to spend money.

Whenever you are less than perfect with your budgeting, don't be too hard on yourself. The idea of your budget is for you to be aware of where your money is going and of where it should be going. Even if you stick to the budget only 2% of the time, you're still better off than not having a budget at all and sticking to it 0% of the time. Every little bit counts.

Authorized Users

If you don't have the credit to get a new credit card or even to extend your current credit line, then your best choice may be to find someone you trust and ask them to become an authorized user on their card. While most people will likely balk at the idea, you may be able to pacify them by explaining that you don't need a copy of their card or have any intent on using it, simply being listed on the card is enough to improve your credit utilization rating. Not only that, but you will also get credit for the on-time payments that this other person makes as well.

Open a New Account

Improving your credit utilization rate is one of the best ways to start rebuilding your credit. If your current credit card company does not want to increase your credit limit, you may way to try applying for another credit card instead. If your credit is not so hot, then your rates are going to be higher, but this won't matter as long as you don't plan on using the card in the first place. Remember, the credit utilization rate is a combination of your total available lines of credit, so this can be a good way to drop your current utilization rate substantially, especially if you won't be able to pay off what you currently owe for a significant period of time.

Keep in mind, however, that if you choose this route, then you are only going to want to apply for one new card every couple of months, especially if you aren't sure if you are going to be approved, as too many hard credit inquiries will only cause your credit score to drop, even if you do end up with a better credit utilization rate as a result. Spreading out these requests will give the inquiries time to drop off naturally and will prevent you from looking desperate to potential lenders, which can also make it more difficult to get a new card.

Increase Your Credit Limit

If you aren't currently in a position to pay down your credit card balance, you can still improve your credit utilization rate by increasing your current credit limit. This is an easy way to improve your credit utilization rate without putting any more money out upfront. However, if you do this, it is important that you don't take advantage of the increased credit line, as if you find yourself up against the limit again, you will be worse off than when you started. Only pursue this option if you have the willpower to avoid racking up extra charges, especially if you are already strapped when it comes to the payments you need to make each month; decreasing your credit utilization limit while also making more late payments is a lateral move at best.

Pay Your Credit Card Bills Twice a Month

If you have a credit card that you use on a regular basis, for example, because it offers you reward points, so much so that you max it out each month, it may actually be hurting your credit even though you pay it off in full at the end of each month. This may be the case due to the way the credit card company reports to the credit bureau; depending on when they report each month, it could show that your credit utilization rate is close to 100 percent depending on what your credit line currently is, thus hurting your credit score. As such, paying off your credit card in two smaller chunks throughout the month can actually help boost your credit without costing you anything extra overall.

Chapter 8. How to Get Out of Debt

Being in debt can hold you back from achieving financial success and happiness. Credit card debts, in particular, are high-interest debts that can pose serious threats to your financial security if allowed to balloon to uncontrollable levels. If you are deeply in debt, you have to face the problem and figure out how you can settle your liabilities as quickly as possible. Work out a repayment plan and be firm on your resolve to get out of debt fast. Stay motivated by constantly reminding yourself of the rewards and benefits of being debt-free.

Here are good reasons why you should pay off your debts fast and stay debt-free for life:

72

1. Being debt-free means you have full control over your finances. You will no longer be at the mercy of your creditors.

2. You will have the money to send your kids to great schools, buy the car you want, or live comfortably in your dream house.

3. Being debt-free means you can use your income to enjoy the finer things in life.

4. Not having to worry about payment and payment due dates reduces anxiety and stress and helps you live a happier and healthier life.

5. By staying out of debt, you will have more money to save and invest in for your retirement.

6. You will be in a better position to prepare for your children's future and deal with life's challenges.

When you set your sights on higher goals, it becomes easier to make sacrifices for a few months or years in exchange for a lifetime of financial security and abundance.

Strategies to Get Out of Debt

How you will settle your debt will depend on your actual financial situation and preferences. Here are proven strategies you can consider when deciding on a payment plan:

1. Make a list of everything you owe. Write down the creditor's name, loan balance, interest rate, and minimum monthly payment required.

2. Sort your debts by amount and interest rate. This will help you assess what credit card debt(s) to prioritize. The most popular method is to put more payment into the debt account with a higher interest rate while paying the minimum amount on the rest of the loans. Once this debt is fully paid, you can continue to use the extra fund to pay off the next card on the list. Using this method can help you pay your debts faster.

3. Another popular strategy is to prioritize payment for the card(s) with the lowest balance while paying the rest of the creditors the minimum amount due. This strategy can be a powerful morale booster. After paying the first target debt in full, you can use the extra fund towards the payment of the card with the next lowest balance.

4. Negotiate with your creditors for a lower rate. If your credit standing is good, banks will likely agree to give you a lower rate instead of losing your account to another creditor. You can use the savings from the reduced interest rate to pay off your principal loan.

5. Consolidating your debts and doing a balance transfer at a significantly lower rate are other options you can consider to free yourself from debt and at the same time help you

save on interest charges. You can do this by asking one of your existing creditors to absorb loan balances from your other cards. Another way to consolidate your loans is by opening a new credit line with a new lender and transferring your loan balances to this new account.

6. Avoid borrowing money to pay your debts or minimum monthly payments. Your goal is to free yourself from debt as fast as possible.

7. Immediately after establishing your emergency fund, prioritize debt payment and use any extra cash, bonuses, or tax refunds to pay down your debts. You will save big on interest charges by using your unexpected funds to settle your debts faster.

8. Don't use your credit cards to purchase new items or pay for your household expenses just because you have managed to free a portion of your card balance.

9. Once you have paid off a credit card debt, have your account closed and cut your credit card. If you must maintain a credit card for contingencies while you're still in the process of building your emergency fund, just maintain one card and keep it in a place where you don't have easy access to it.

10. Don't use your home as a guarantee for the payment of your credit card balances. Remember that credit cards are

unsecured debts and are given to you on the basis of your credit scores. If you fail to pay, you risk losing your home.

11. You can negotiate with your creditors and banks directly. You don't have to hire the services of a debt settlement company or financial agents to arrange a balance transfer. Educate yourself on simple financial calculations and be able to compare banks' offers on your own.

12. Constantly visualize yourself as living the life of your dreams because you have finally conquered debt.

13. Finally, to pay off your debts faster, free off more funds by controlling your expenses and making more money.

Chapter 9.Right Mindset for Credit Management

H aving the mindset of a lender allows you to manage your money in a way that makes you a good credit candidate in the eyes of lenders. Apply the following tips when handling your finances to help you develop the mindset of a lender.

Do Your Research

Knowing how money works will go a long way toward helping you maintain your credit report's good standing. Keep your good credit score from dipping by reading books on finance management. It helps if you have knowledge of how your accounts and loans work so that handling them will be easier for you. When you take steps to understand how money works in general, you equip yourself with tools that will help you make wiser financial decisions and avoid a bad credit rating.

Confirm Your Closed Accounts

It doesn't matter if they are bank accounts, credit accounts, or even your utility company accounts – what does matter is that you ask for a written confirmation for every account you close. Make sure that each closed account has been fully paid up. It helps if you follow up with your bank or credit card company a couple of months afterward to confirm that the accounts have been closed.

Know How Lenders View You

Your credit score is not the only thing that lenders will often examine in your credit report. They also take the time to look at other financial indicators such as your employment history, your income, and your savings. Work on keeping these details in order to help you maintain your good credit score and achieve good overall credit, especially since there are a number of lenders who employ their methods of computing credit scores.

Constantly Update Your Records, Including Your Current Address

Making sure that all your records are updated regularly helps you keep your lenders and financial managers up-to-date as well. It helps to keep all of your financial information in one folder at home, including and especially your current address. It will serve as a reminder to contact your creditors in case you move and give them your new address. This will prevent the problems of not getting your bills, being unable to pay them, and seeing your credit score go down as a result.

Aim for Stability

As much as possible, do not move around too much. Moving frequently results in your having to switch banks. This prevents you from developing long-term relationships with any of them, and this has a negative effect on your credit score and credit report. On the same note, it helps to avoid changing jobs too often. To some lenders, frequent job changes are an indication that you are likely to make loan defaults or go off with the money without paying. It also helps to avoid frequently changing your credit accounts and credit companies. Doing so prevents you from building a good credit relationship with any of them and could cause you to have a low credit rating.

Keep the Lines of Credit Communication Open

As soon as a problem in your finances crops up, take steps to talk to your creditors. This will give them reassurance about your being responsible as a borrower, and this helps to prevent your credit report from being negatively affected. All it takes is calling them over the phone and arranging to have your payment schedules adjusted, as well as getting your penalties waived free of charge.

Chapter 10. Best Credit Repair Companies and Why I Should Use Their Services

Credit repair agencies often make promises such as "you will be in debt" or "your credit will be restored quickly." However, they usually can't do anything more for you than you can do on your own, either with the help of someone else or on your own. Additionally, some of their promises might be impossible to keep. Let's take an example. A credit repair agency may argue that it will "remove this bankruptcy from your credit report"; while under Ontario law, bankruptcy can remain on your credit report for seven years. No one, not even a fee-based credit repair agency, can have the bankruptcy in question withdrawn before these seven years have elapsed.

Some credit repair agencies offer to improve your credit rating by giving you a loan that you would pay off over time. Beware: you might never see the money from such a loan, as these agencies use the loaned money to pay the fees they charge you for this "service." Maintaining a good credit report is like presenting a beautiful school report to your parents: it gives you bargaining power to get what you want. Except that instead of having the right to take the minivan for the weekend, with the credit report, you can buy yourself one.

It is also a determining factor when shopping for a mortgage and financing. This can lead to a low interest rate and optimal borrowing conditions. Also, some employers and homeowners will require it.

Since it is difficult to escape it, it is in your interest to pay attention to it. To finally understand how it works and know the best tips for a file that will make you the darling of financial institutions, read on.

How does it work? Here are the essentials to enter the patent.

Periodically, lenders and service providers (cellular, internet, etc.) submit your account information (balances, payments, limits, open and close dates, terms, etc.) to Equifax and TransUnion. These credit reporting agencies put it all together and give you a score ranging from 300 to 900, as well as a rating ranging from 1 to 9.

A high score indicates that you are in good financial health and that you can probably be trusted. I say "probably" because the credit report is not a perfect, omniscient tool. If you've owed your mom money since you bought her minivan in 2019, the agencies don't know.

The "1" rating means that an account is paid according to the terms. For each month of delay, the odds go up by one point to the maximum of "5" representing more than 120 days of arrears. An account sent to a collection agency or included in a bankruptcy is usually assigned a rating of "9". The rating "7" indicates that the account is the subject of a specific payment arrangement with a creditor.

Making the Best of Credit Bureaus

It is important to learn that all three credit bureaus have sensitive financial data. However, there is no method to prevent lenders and collection entities from sharing your information with the above companies. You can limit any possible problems associated with the credit bureaus by evaluating your credit reports annually and acting immediately in case you notice some errors. It is also good to monitor your credit cards and other open credit products to ensure that no one is misusing the accounts. If you have a card that you do not often use, sign up for alerts on that card so that you get notified if any transactions happen and regularly review statements for your active tickets. Next, if you notice any signs of fraud or theft, you can choose to place a credit freeze with the three credit bureaus and be diligent in tracking the activity of your credit card in the future.

The credit bureau company is also dominated by three major players as the rating agency, namely: Experian, Equifax, and

TransUnion. A fascinating feature of the credit bureau's business model is the exchange of information. Banks, retailers, finance companies, and landlords send information to the credit bureaus for free, and then the credit bureaus contact them and sell consumer information back to them.

Credit bureaus are responsible for packaging and analyzing consumer credit reports obtained directly from credit scores. Unlike credit ratings issued in letters, credit scores have theirs issued in numbers, usually between 350–850. Your credit score affects the loan amounts you can pay for the debt and sometimes your rental and employment opportunities. You can access your credit report once a year from each credit bureau. Both rating agencies and credit bureaus are heavily regulated and have been under scrutiny since the Great Recession from 2007 to 2009.

How the Bureaus Get Their Information

To learn how the score gets calculated, we need to learn about all the different inputs of your score, aka where the bureaus get their info. You may have many factors that report information to the credit bureaus or none. Credit cards are called revolving accounts or revolving debt by the credit bureaus. Each month payments and balances are reported, as well as any late payments. This means that any cards that have your name on them will also report to all the bureaus. This includes cards that belong to a spouse or parent. If you are an authorized user on the account, it gets reported on your credit no matter what. Many people have their credit ruined by a spouse or parent going into bankruptcy or not paying their credit card bills. If your name is on any credit card that belongs to people that may not pay their bills, ask them to take your name off immediately! Installment loans also report information to the credit bureaus. If you went down to your local Sears and financed a washer/dryer set by putting up a down payment, that is an installment loan. The details of these loans are all reported; the total balance, as well as the timeliness and amounts of your monthly payments. If you have mortgages or student loans, that information does get reported. Total amounts due, total paid so far, and the status of monthly payments is all reported. This information is kept track of and organized in their databases.

Chapter 11.Best Way to Handle Student Loans or Medical Collections

You might have been untiring in paying off your student loans every month, but somehow you missed a couple of payments because you fell into tough times.

Do you have to be disciplined for unintended circumstances? Can you ever rebound from a bad credit score?

When you're in a tight financial position, it can sound like you're never going to get out of the slump.

That cannot be much further from the facts. Not only can you get out of that seemingly impossible pit, then you're going to live and tell others about it, so they're going to be inspired by your experience.

So after a student loan default, are you able to restore your credit?

Let's discuss five effective ways to restore credit after defaulting on a student loan.

Rehabilitate Your Loans

Your credit report will show up being in debt on your student loans. Clearly, as this is a derogatory element, it will substantially downgrade your credit score.

One way you can get your credit report removed by default is by rehabilitating your loans. Ultimately, because of that simple fact, this is the easiest way to rebuild credit after a student loan default!

Once you rehabilitate your debt, you come to an agreement with the loan servicer to pay a small monthly sum between 9 and 12 months for anywhere. When you follow this plan and pay the monthly amount on time each month, your credit report will be taken off by default.

That will help you get some points back on your credit score.

Consolidate Your Loans

The next thing you can do is merge your debts in your attempt to restore your reputation.

If you have federal loans from different servicers, consolidating your debts will make your payments smoother.

For example, the Direct Consolidation Mortgage would allow you to make just one monthly payment on your federal loans, rather than several payments. It makes things easier and you'll be more likely to pay them back sooner.

Alternatively, if you are in a qualified occupation, the Direct Consolidation Loan gives you access to the Public Service Loan Forgiveness plan.

One advantage you will find with this system is that the interest rate appears to be smaller than when you borrow private loans because it is controlled by the government.

Use Income-Based Repayment Programs

This can also help rebuild your credit after a default by paying off your student loans using a revenue-based repayment plan.

You will base these payments on your current income. If you can make payments in a timely manner each month, your accounts will remain current and will not go into default.

Use a Secured Credit Card

It's usually easier to get a secured credit card than a free credit card. This is because you are making a deposit that serves as your credit limit on the card.

Your credit score will continue to improve as long as you make monthly payments on your secured credit card on time.

During your "rebuilding" phase, once you have used a secured card for a year or two, you can get rid of it and use a regular credit card.

Your Debt Ratio: Keep It Below 30%

As a general rule of thumb, it helps to build up your credit score by keeping your debt below 30% of your total available credit.

Whether you use a protected visa or a regular credit card, this rule of thumb is a safe one to remember at all times.

Keep Tabs of Your FICO Score

Your FICO score is your billing habits' financial fingerprint. This shorthand creditworthiness, reduced to a numeral (from 300 to 850, the higher, the better), allows lenders to determine whether to accept you for loans and credit cards and what interest rate to charge. Employers also use it to learn about work candidates, and homeowners and car insurers review potential policyholders' credit scores to assess their premiums.

Credit scores generally rise with age: 42% of people in their 60s have credit scores of 780 or higher, and 55% of those over 70 have credit scores of 780 or higher.

In general, credit scores rise with age: 42% of people in their 60s have a credit score of 780 or higher, and 55% of those over 70 have a score of 780 or higher.

Lately, the tracking of your FICO score (or equivalent credit score) has become very painless. Many banks and credit card firms offer monthly and online customer statements. Discover was one of the first, but Bank of America, Barclaycard, Chase, and Citi were among the others to follow. Secure yourself from the theft of identity.

In addition to monitoring your FICO ratings, take the appropriate steps to ensure that you do not become a victim of identity theft. Your ability to obtain credit is jeopardized when someone uses your name, address, Social Security number, or other identifiers to purchase or open credit card accounts.

There are a few ways to hold identity thieves at bay:

- Shred deposit, credit card and other accounts. Better still, sign up for online statements to stop robbers from stealing your mail or digging through your garbage.

- Periodically check bank and credit card statements for any irregularities.

- Never give personal financial details by phone to an individual or business you don't know about.

- Do not use public Wi-Fi to access your bank or credit card websites. Identity hackers can capture the data electronically if you do so.

- File your tax return immediately if you don't already have one. Identity criminals have been busy filing false tax returns and making tax refunds in the last few years.

Check Your Credit Report Regularly

Request a free copy of your credit report at least once a year to search for fraud.

The Keys to Successfully Rid Debt

Charge More than the Minimum Fee

Make sure you still spend more than your full credit card payments, overdraft, or line of credit. If you make your minimum credit card payments on a monthly basis, it will literally take a long time to pay off your balance. If you want to repay off your balance fast, pay as much extra as you can. An additional $50 each month is going to help.

Spend Less Than You're Going to Spend

Most of us have wishes and needs that are greater than our paychecks. You may have heard the old saying, "You can have almost everything you want; you just can't afford anything you want." A lot of people fall into debt and remain in debt because they prefer to buy what they want when they want to.

Another crucial way to spend less is to pay in cash rather than on credit. McDonald's also found that customers spend 56% more in their restaurants when they pay with credit rather than cash. Studies have indicated that when people use credit, they spend 100 percent more on vending machines or on event tickets. Overall, studies seem to suggest that people prefer to spend at least 15% more on everything they buy using credit. If we apply this idea to a typical Canadian household that is actually purchasing something with credit cards to earn points or get cashback, they will possibly save well over $3,000 a year if they just purchased cash things instead (the points or cashback will only be worth $400 at best).

Even if your savings aren't as good as this example, you might be able to see the point. If you wish to be debt-free, leave your cards at home, use cash, and don't buy anything with credit until you've paid down your debt to the amount you're working towards.

Pay the Most Expensive Loans First

When you've paid off the first, most costly debt, take all the money you paid out on your first debt and concentrate it on the second, most expensive debt. Continue this process while you pay off each of your debts, and you'll last be left with your least expensive debt to pay off. This plan will keep you safe from debt fast, and you'll feel motivated to see your progress.

Buy a Better-Used Car Instead of a New Model

A popular personal finance radio host, Dave Ramsey, once said, "A new $28,000 car would lose around $17,000 in value in the first four years you own it."

The lesson for you here is that you can save yourself thousands if you buy a better-used car instead of a new one. The money you save will help you get out of debt a lot faster.

Consider Being a Single Car Household

If your family has two vehicles, consider getting rid of one and walking to work, bus, or carpool. You can literally save dollars in thousands a year by utilizing only one vehicle. The typical car owner spends more than $9,000 a year maintaining and running his car. If you use this money to pay off your mortgage, it's going to make a big difference. However, instead of going cold turkey and selling your second car right away, try the test of driving this concept first. Park your vehicle for a bit, drop insurance to fun only, and see if you're in transit, biking, cycling or carpooling. If you plan to sell your second car, even an occasional taxi ride or the rental car won't amount to nearly as much as you will pay to retain your second vehicle forever. If there is a possibility that transit will work for you, this alternative alone is sometimes 80 percent cheaper than owning and driving a car.

Save on Groceries to Help Repay Off Debt Faster

To save more cash and pay off your debt more easily, consider storing up grocery stores while they're on sale, or go a step further and store them when they're on sale, and then miss a grocery store every month and live off the food you've stored. You can store non-perishable food, such as canned goods, cereal, and items that you can freeze, like bread and meat. Filling your cupboards when grocery stores are on sale and then missing one grocery store per month will save you up to 25% of your annual grocery bill. A family of four would be able to save $2,300 to $2,900 a year by doing this. Applying this kind of savings to your debts would certainly put you ahead in the long run!

The secret to this approach is to watch for sales, just to shop when grocery stores are on sale and to freeze food properly. When you miss a grocery store, you'll always need to buy perishable food like milk, fruit, and vegetables, but hopefully, you can skip the rest of what you would usually buy. If you can't miss a shop once a month, try it once every other month. It can also save you a very good amount of money.

Get Your Second Job and Pay Off Your Debt Vigorously

Having a second job, or even an extra shift or two, is a common way for many people to pay down their debts. This doesn't work for everybody, but if you can make it work, you might be debt-free in a few years. You are required to contribute all of your extra profits to the repayment of your debt. Often, working extra shifts or hours doesn't need to be permanent. When your loans have been paid off, you will see the scale back again.

You might also consider producing some extra money to pay off your debt by capitalizing on a hobby you love or a skill set you may have. For example, if you are an effective writer, suggest freelance articles for blogs, journals, freelance websites or media outlets. If you're crafty, consider selling your creative works on Etsy. If you're a handy person, see if you can pick up any extra jobs (you may even be able to find websites that can help link you to people who need your skills).

Some people still use their homes to produce some extra cash. Is it possible for you to rent your basement, rent a storage space in your house, rent a room in your home, or take a student with you for some extra income?

Track Your Expenses and Recognize Areas That Should Be Cut Back

For some people, doing this will save them about as much money as doing part-time jobs. You're not going to know how much you can save until you try it. Track what you're really spending — not what you think you're going to spend a month. If you're not honest with yourself in this exercise, it's not going to work, but most people are shocked by what they find out about their spending. When you know your spending patterns, you need to be able to find places where you can cut back. Allocate the money you "find" to pay off your debts.

Get Your Consolidation Loan

See if your bank or credit union will help you combine all your consumer loans into one loan with one payment at a lower interest rate. This may be a valuable first step in getting your debt paid off.

Savings isn't usually the first thing someone thinks about debt, so if you don't have savings, you're likely to have to use your credit cards part way through your loan again and end up getting more debt. The end result could have you in the same position as before or worse off. The U.S. bank, which has checked all its debt consolidation loans for a number of years, has found that more than 70% of the people who borrowed a debt consolidation loan from them are not financially better off after repaying their loans. This happened because these people did not fix the fundamental issue of spending more than they had gained.

So, the trick to benefiting from a consolidation loan and making it an efficient tool is to use a spending plan (budget) to ensure that you keep your spending under control and set aside some funds every month for emergencies or unplanned expenses that will eventually occur.

Refinancing Your Mortgage

If you get your own house, you can have enough equity to combine all of your mortgage debts. If you don't have a lot of equity in your house, extra mortgage insurance premiums can be costly. Make sure you weigh all of your choices and seek advice from someone other than your lender (because they have a vested interest in getting you to choose this option). If a regular bank or credit union can't help you out, don't hurry to find the first home equity loan company willing to lend you the money. Instead, first have a discussion with an approved, non-profit Credit Counselor. You could have better choices than refinancing your home that you don't know about. They will help you analyze all your choices and come up with the best strategy to move you forward and achieve your financial goals.

If you refinance your home and combine your mortgage obligations, you need to think of the new mortgage as the debt restructuring loans we discussed above. It's super important that you keep your expenses in line with your income (following the budget is typically the easiest way to do this) and allocate money to savings every month. If you don't save some money, you'll still be tempted to borrow more when an "emergency" comes up. Using your house as a bank machine repeatedly will set you up to face retirement with a lot of debt, no assets, and no savings. If this is something that you're dealing with, read on.

Talk to the Credit Counselor-It's Free

If you're in debt and just struggling to make any progress in paying down your debt, begin by talking to the Credit Counsellor. Find out what services are ready to help you deal with your debt. A reputable credit counselor will clarify all of your choices and help you select the one that makes the most sense to you in your situation. Some people don't know what they need to know about the debt reduction services of non-profit credit counseling agencies, but others are glad that they took the time to find out before it was too late. Talking with a non-profit Credit Counselor about your choices is confidential, non-judgmental and typically free of charge.

Positive Complaints from Credit Repair

The best way to make a credit repair success is to know what to expect from the process before you get started. If you get into it with an exaggerated idea of what you're going to do, you're inevitably going to be frustrated in the end. Realistic standards can go a long way in the field of credit repair (and finance in general).

So, it's a matter of understanding which things in your credit report actually qualify for a good dispute.

Because the mechanism is structured to ensure that the records are accurate, the types of things that may usually be excluded by credit repair are those that are, in any way, wrong. This involves things that are inaccurate, false, obsolete or unsubstantiated.

- *Wrong Items:* The simplest type of object to be contested is one that is absolutely incorrect. This involves simple mistakes, such as spelling errors or misreported numbers, which can cause misunderstanding or credit problems. For example, if the decimal point is in the wrong position, it could look like you have much more debt than you should have. In certain cases, basic errors require no effort for the

96

credit bureau to review and can be corrected in a very short period of time.

- *Obsolete Items:* Another form of contested object that is usually easy to repair is old-fashioned items. Many derogatory items will only stay on your credit report for a certain period of time until they need to be deleted. Hard credit investigations, for example, last up to two years, while overdue payments can last up to seven years. However, once these products reach their maximum age, they should be deleted from your record automatically, or you can file a dispute to get them deleted.

- *Fraudulent Items:* If you've ever been a victim of identity theft, you might end up with fraudulent accounts on your credit reports. Although these accounts can appear genuine at first, further examination may sometimes expose their sinister roots. In addition to filing disputes to delete fraudulent accounts from your reports, be sure to disclose any cases of identity theft immediately.

- *Unsubstantiated Items:* The last of the commonly contested items are those accounts in the records that cannot be verified by the information providers. If they cannot prove that the debt or negative mark really belongs to you, the credit bureaus will reject the object.

As a consequence, one or two of your credit reports might contain disputed items that do not appear in the other reports. Since you cannot foresee the credit report(s) the creditor would use to assess your credit risk, all three of your credit reports should be in good shape to avoid future credit defaults.

Advanced Guide to Credit Repair

The Lower Debt-to-Credit Ratio

Having a lower debt-to-credit ratio holds the secret to getting the "credit attitude" right. This will demonstrate your ability to manage balances and pay overtime and your creditworthiness, which is most profitable to lenders because they make money mainly through interest and not through annual fees. You'll be able to get a loan more quickly by getting a lower debt-to-credit ratio.

Subscribe to Subprime Product Cards

Sub Prime Product Cards can be used to increase the high credit cap and reduce their debt-to-credit ratio. However, most of us have mistaken the advantages of this card because there are a large number of companies advertising it. When you learn how they work, you easily understand why they have been the target of a lot of misappropriation.

Piggybacking

Almost any credit card or credit account would allow the primary account holder to add to what is known as the "Approved Consumer" or "Secondary Account Holder." Individuals with excellent credit ratings can have their full history posted on the credit report of the registered users.

Here are the three little secrets that Lawyers and Credit Repair Clinics don't want you to know:

Secret 1

When it comes to the derogatory marks on your credit, the big secret they don't want you to know is that the only derogatory facts that can stay on your credit report are not what is accurate, but what the credit bureaus can show to be accurate.

Secret 2

They know that the problem of proof falls on your creditors and the credit bureaus, and not you.

Secret 3

They understand how to write conflicts that make it very difficult for the creditors and credit bureaus to prove this presumption of evidence. Anything that your creditors and credit bureaus can't prove must be permanently excluded from your credit reports-it's the rule!

Chapter 12. Effective Strategies to Rehabilitate Your Finances

Hire an Expert

You can manage your company because you are quite intelligent, and in some way, everyone is. However, no matter how good you are, it is always nice to have an expert's opinions, especially in technical cases like this. You have learned hard lessons when your credit score drastically fell and you struggled to get it up, so it isn't such a bad idea to hear a couple of incisive words from a colossus. They would help with your budget, plans, financial decisions, and so forth. Services like these are sometimes charged and sometimes free, depending on the organization's motive or the person you are approaching. You may hire a credit or financial counselor, an economist, or a bankruptcy attorney, among other specialists.

Work on Your History

Since you are starting over, it is always a good idea to review your history. You should find out what you did wrong in each case and what was right and should have been enforced in your transactions. You should also learn about terms convenient for your business, policies you can subscribe to, and those you shouldn't ever consider, no matter how juicy they seem. You should be on the lookout for errors you didn't note, who charged exorbitantly, whom you can bank on for further business deals, and so on.

Be Updated on Your Credit Score

It is a new season, and you want to enjoy all the blessings it brings. One way you can do this is to start monitoring your credit report so it doesn't ever go bad again. No matter how bad it seems already, you are bound to get the best out of it when you are updated with your credit scores and your credit report in general.

You must think about your credit position and make informed decisions in your finances every single time. Gradually, you can boost your credit scores this way. Besides, you need to keep your eyes on the credit report and your credit bureaus.

You deserve a spick-and-span record this time, and you shouldn't avoid lapses that can ruin that. So, be updated on your credit information and consider that each time you make financial decisions.

Do Not Close Your Old Accounts

Whether your accounts have become delinquent or have gotten to a point wherein you don't want to associate with them anymore, it is always recommended that you still keep them open in some way.

Keeping accounts open can serve as an advantage in further credit transactions to prove your experience with loans.

However, if you must close an account, be sure there is no debt or balance to be covered in it as that can be a big minus to your new account. It is highly recommended that you avoid creating new credit records at this point.

Reach Out to Your Creditors

Now, this is interesting. Many people do not see the need to reach out to their creditors after their loans have been activated. Especially if they can afford the charges and there seems no reason to be in touch. However, that's not right. There can be cases wherein you can't pay your monthly dues. Sometimes, you may have huge plans or investments that can't wait till the coming month, and your best way to hit this is your monthly debt. If you are in touch with them, establish that you appreciate their business interaction and do not mind relating them beyond the current contract. You will be glad you did because you can count on them to be lenient at such moments and find some way to ensure your credit score is not affected. Many business transactions are conducted on the grounds of a good relationship between the key figures in the business.

Be Patient

Your credit score didn't deteriorate in hours; you should expect to rebuild it to take some time. The different steps you take will not yield many positive results immediately, certainly not as much as you'd like, but it's no reason to despair.

It is certainly possible to build it again, and it will happen if you are consistent. Do not mind how long the process seems – it always works by consistency, as Harry Hans of Financial times would say.

Avoid Unnecessary Credits

You surely remember that the federal court on Bankruptcy declared in 2013 that over 70% of unsecured debts are incurred on purchases that could be avoided. You don't want to add a penny to that percentage. It is why you should avoid purchasing items that do not appear in your budget. You should also limit the rate at which you explore markets and rake home some niceties, courtesy of your credit card. You can hit a nice score again if you take those tips. None of these are new principles. They are all simple and practical, so ensure you always remember them.

Chapter 13.Financial Freedom

Financial freedom is a concept that people love to think about but rarely feel like they can reach. This will help you reach financial freedom by using tips and habits that can be incorporated into your life.

What Is Meant by Financial Freedom?

Financial freedom has no set definition. However, it typically means that you are living comfortably and saving for retirement and in general. It can also mean that you have an emergency reserve set up. In general, financial freedom can mean whatever you want it to mean for you. For example, a prior college student may not think that financial freedom includes repayment of all his student loans. This is because, at least in this day and age, a college student who needs to pay in his own way realizes that he will always be paying off his student loans. However, he might feel that student loans are the only debt he should have. Therefore, being able to pay off credit cards or medical bills leads them to financial freedom.

Other people may feel that financial freedom means they are no longer tied down to a job. They are able to live off of their savings or a passive income, and they are able to retire and enjoy life through traveling.

Credit Cards and Financial Freedom - Is It Safe?

One of the biggest questions people have when it comes to financial freedom is whether they can have any credit card accounts in their name. While you may not owe anything on your credit cards (in fact, you might only owe one that you pay off in full every month), is this still financial freedom? In general, this is completely determined by your definition of financial freedom. However, if you ever find yourself not being able to pay off your credit card every month, this is not financial freedom. In most cases, financial freedom does mean you no longer have any debt or, at least, that you are free from unnecessary debt, such as credit cards.

Most people are quick to state that financial freedom and credit cards do not go together simply because they are not safe with each other. This is due to the fact that it is often easy to fall back into thinking you can pay the amount off everything each month and then you become unable to do so. In general, people who reach financial freedom feel that credit cards allow for more of a trap and keep them from reaching financial freedom.

The Best Habits to Help You Reach and Protect Your Financial Freedom

When it comes to financial freedom, there are dozens of habits and tips that people provide in order to help you reach your financial freedom. It is important to note that because financial freedom can vary depending on the person's definition, some tips and habits might work for you while others may not. You need to find the ones that work best for you, not the ones that other people say are the best.

Make a Budget

Making and keeping a budget is one of the first steps everyone should take while heading towards financial freedom. Even though you might find yourself changing your budget now and then, as you will add or delete bills or receive a different income, you always want to follow it. Not only will this help you in reaching your financial freedom, but continuing to follow your budget will also protect your financial freedom.

Furthermore, creating a monthly budget can make sure that all your bills are being paid and you know exactly where your money is going. This will help you know where you can decrease your spending, which will allow you to save more. There are a lot of great benefits when it comes to creating and sticking with a household budget.

Set Up Automatic Savings Account

If you work for an organization that will automatically place a certain percentage of your check into a savings account, take advantage of this. It gives you the idea that you never had the money to begin with, which means you don't plan for it and you won't find yourself taking the money out of savings unless you need it for an emergency. Furthermore, you can set up a separate savings account where this money will go. You may rarely see this account, however, you want to make sure your money is deposited and everything looks good in your account. But the point of this account if you don't touch it, even if you have an emergency. Instead, you will create a different account for an emergency basis.

The other idea of this is you pay yourself first. This is often something that people don't think about because they are more worried about paying off their debt.

Keep Your Credit in Mind without Obsessing Over It

Your credit score is important, but it is not the most important thing in the world. People often fall into the trap of becoming obsessed over their credit score, especially when trying to improve it. One factor to remember is that your credit score is typically only updated occasionally. Therefore, you can decide to set time aside every quarter to check on your credit report. When you do this, you not only want to check your score, but you also want to check what the credit bureaus are reporting. Like you want to make sure everything is correct in your bank account, you want to do the same thing for your credit report.

It Is Fine to Live Below Your Means

One of the biggest factors of financial freedom and being able to maintain it is you can make your bills and comfortably live throughout the month. In order to do this, you need to make sure that the money coming into your home is more than the money going out. In other words, you want to live below your means.

This is often difficult for a lot of people because they want to have what other people have. They want to have the newer vehicles, the bigger boat, the newest grill, or anything else. People like to have what their friends and neighbors have. However, one-factor people don't think about is that their friends and neighbors probably don't have financial freedom. Therefore, you want to take a moment to think about what is more important for you. Would you rather be in debt like your friends or would you rather have financial freedom?

Speak with a Financial Advisor

Sometimes the best step we can take when we are working towards financial freedom is to talk with a financial advisor. They can often give up information and help us with a budget, ways to make sure that we get the most out of our income, and also tell us where we might be spending more money than we should. Furthermore, they can help you figure out what the best investments are, which are always helpful when you are looking at financial freedom. At the same time, they can help you plan for your retirement, which is one of the biggest ways you will be able to remain financially free.

Completely Pay Off Your Credit Cards

If you are high-interest credit cards, which is often the case, you want to make sure that you pay these off every month. Therefore, your credit card spending should become part of your budget. What this means is you don't want to use your credit card for whatever you feel like. Instead, you want to create a list of when

108

you can and when you can't use your credit card. For example, you might agree that it is fine in emergency situations or during Christmas shopping. You might also feel that you can use it during trips because it has travel insurance attached to it. Whatever you decide, you want to make sure you follow.

Track Your Spending

Along with making sure you follow your budget, you also want to track your spending. There are several reasons for this. First, it will help you make sure that your budget is on track. We often forget about automatic bills that are paid monthly or don't realize how much we really spend every month. These factors can make our budget off, which can cause an obstacle when you are working to reaching and keeping your financial freedom.

Fortunately, there are many apps that you can download, many of them are free, which will allow you to track your spending easily. Some of these apps include Mint or Personal Capital. These apps typically give you all the information you need and will automatically tell you how much you are spending and how much income you still hold at the end of the month. Most of these apps will also give you charts to help you see your spending habits in a different way.

Continue Your Education

Another way to stay on top of your financial freedom is to become educated when it comes to your budget, spending, taxes, and anything else to do with your finances. This doesn't mean that you have to go back to school and earn a degree. You can do your own research or take online classes, some of which you will find are low-cost to free. You can also look into webinars that people hold.

You can also help yourself when it comes to investing in the stock market or anything else. There are always several classes you can take online, which only have a few sessions or ways you can learn when you have the time. In fact, if you want to invest but don't know what to do or where to begin, one of your best options is to take a class.

Make Sure to Keep Your Mindset

This is a mindset that you will want to continue to have while you are living financially free. With this mindset, you will not only feel grateful for where you are in life, but you will also remember where you once were. This will help you work towards protecting your financial freedom instead of falling back into credit card debt.

Of course, you can adjust your mindset the way you want to once you reach financial freedom. However, you will want to make sure that you keep your mindset positive. After all, a positive mindset makes you believe that you can accomplish anything.

Make Sure You Write down What Financial Freedom Means to You

Financial freedom can mean something different to you than it means to someone else. Because of this, you have to think about what it truly means to you. Whatever you feel it means, it is important to write this down. This will allow you to turn back to what financial freedom means to you when you find yourself struggling and feeling like you can't gain your financial freedom.

At the same time, it is also helpful to take time to write down your goals. Think of what you want to accomplish on your road to

110

financial freedom. You can also think about what you want to do after you have reached financial freedom. Give yourself goals to work towards, as this will help you stay on track better.

Developing Wealth

Throughout the years, through a research study, interviews, I've discovered that individuals who have an excellent deal of wealth and individuals who preserve a favorable capital have actually established a favorable wealth awareness.

I keep in mind talking to a buddy who owns a chain of hotels across the United States and is now expanding into Canada and overseas. He explained he had actually originated from an immigrant family; his daddy worked as an accounting professional and later opened a store while his mother put herself through school, eventually ending up being a nursing sister. However, my point is he didn't have a family that provided him with a million dollars to start his endeavor. Rather, he began off working for his father, ultimately took control of the company, bought another, made it a success, offered it and purchased another till he got his first hotel just outside Dallas.

Let's define positive wealth consciousness as a method of believing that you can and will generate income. It involves thinking that it is your right to generate income and create wealth. It needs that you concentrate on all the great things that your wealth can do for you and those around you. If you have wealth, you will assist more individuals, and it means understanding that. It suggests putting your ego aside- not wanting wealth so that you can flaunt and say: "Look at me, I'm rich." Rather it suggests saying: "Yes, I have a lot of wealth which enables me to take care of many people, including my household and all those that I help when I invest my money."

You will invest your money, let's face it, the more you have, the more you will spend.

In order to bring in wealth, you need to take very first a look at where you are now and then create a realistic approach for a couple of months, a year, or more years. Perhaps you are indebted due to the task- intending to have a million dollars in 6 months is not being extremely realistic. Rather your very first priority must be to get and get a job out of debt. If you currently have a job and you want to make more cash, then offer yourself some sensible targets for the next 3 months, 6 months, year, and 5 years. Now I understand a few of you will say it's tough to generate the income, I do not know what to do to make more money, I'm in debt and don't understand how to go out. For each issue there is an option for a solution, otherwise, we would not have problems. Concentrate on finding an option. Train your mind to focus on the service. Begin to forward messages to your conscious mind for a solution. Do this frequently, and you'll get answers. The money will not fall from the sky, but you will be guided to it. How Do You Train Your Mind? You initially focus on what you desire. Let's state you wish to find a task- you start to proclaim that you know what to do to find a task.

What You Can Do to Attract Wealth

There are a variety of techniques you can employ to attract wealth, regardless of your situation. You have to get your mind to work for you and not versus you. Here's a little exercise you can do. Get a notepad and a pen. Now begin thinking of generating income or enhancing your financial resources. Jot down all the thoughts that come to mind when you think of enhancing your finances or creating wealth. Be sincere – then you will see this list. Keep going until you feel you have had to satisfy. Keep contributing to that list throughout the day. Then when you feel you have got enough - have a look at what you wrote. Highlight the thoughts that are favorable and circle the ideas that are negative. How lots of are you negative? Any negative thought you have about money or to improve your finances is connected to a belief that you have about money and only works against you. If you believe it's challenging to make more cash, you'll only have problems when it concerns making cash. Why? Due to the fact that your subconscious mind is just going to develop your truth based on your beliefs. If these beliefs are bad or great for you, it doesn't care. It simply acts upon your guidelines, and those guidelines are your beliefs and thoughts. Modify your beliefs, and you change your life.

The Importance of Investing

Investing your money gives you a chance to grow your money and even make more than what you have. However, not everyone who decides to invest their money makes profits; some have lost tons of money in the process. There is a different way to invest your money, and this will introduce you to some of the most common strategies for investment.

Online investing can be a quick and convenient method that is more affordable than other methods. But before you can handle your online investment, you need to ask yourself several questions.

Online investing is designed for everyone. By choosing this option, you hold the responsibility to research all investments and make all investment decisions regarding your online account. If you

113

don't feel okay as that kind of investor, you could be comfortable working with a financial advisor. If you like to manage your investment portfolio and feel secure that you have enough knowledge, you may decide to go with online investment.

Stop Spending

If you can't stop spending money that you don't have, this book will only temporarily fix your problems, if it is even able to do that. If you have a habit of living out of your means and buying things you cannot afford, this is your chance to fix that. If you want to fix your credit and improve your life financially, you must take care of these things. So, sit tight, make a budget, and find something that works, and cut up those maxed-out credit cards if you have to.

Budgeting and Saving

When you budget, you get the chance to single out and eliminate unnecessary spendings, such as penalties, late fees, and interests. These little savings can increase with time.

A budget refers to a plan that takes into account your monthly cash flow and outflow. This is a snapshot of what you own and what you expect to spend, and which will allow you to realize your financial goals by assisting you in highlighting your saving and spending.

Creating a budget is the most crucial aspect of financial planning. The amount of money you have doesn't indicate how much money you make, but instead, it is how effective your budgeting is. If you want to take care of your finances, then you will have to understand where your money is flowing to. Contrary to popular belief that budgeting is hard, it isn't, and it doesn't eliminate the fun from your life. A budget will save you from an unexpected financial crisis and a life of debt.

Monitor Your Expenses and Income

The first thing to building a budget is to determine the amount of money you have and what you are spending it on. By monitoring your expenses, you will manage to classify how you spend your money. Planning how you spend your money is critical because you can tell how much you want to spend in every category. You can monitor your income and expenses by creating a journal, spreadsheet, or cash book. Every time you make money, you can monitor it as income, and every time you spend money, you can track it as an expense.

If you use a debit card, try to track back three months of your spending to get a comprehensive picture of your expenditure.

Evaluate Your Income

The next stage is to evaluate your income. You can do this by computing the amount of income you get via gifts, scholarships, etc.

Determine Your Expenses

Fixed expenses, sales, and bills have the same price every month. The fixed expenses comprise car payments, internet, and rent. Variable expenses refer to costs that change, such as utilities and groceries.

Be sure to include payments of debt in your budget. Find out the amount that you can contribute towards your debts to make sure that you are on the correct path to financial stability. Handling debts and savings go hand in hand.

Building a Saving Strategy

It is quite easy to forget to save money. Keep in mind that you always pay yourself first. Give it a try using 10-20% of your income savings. Since savings increase, you can choose to include money that you didn't spend in the budget to save.

Many people know how to manage the little money they get when the month ends, but they find it hard to save when they have a tight budget. If you look at finance articles online, you will see different types of saving methods, right from freezing all spending to packing your lunch for a month.

Conclusion

Now, you have the information that will help you build better credit and increase your credit score. Some of these strategies may not work for your situation or if you have already been employing them. Hopefully, you found a few new strategies to try and will be able to achieve the status you wish to have in your credit scores.

Anyone who has not nourished a long history with numerous types of credit may also be having trouble gaining a score above 800. However, you have fewer steps to take to get your credit scores higher. You simply need to be paying attention to the credit types you have, ensuring that you open new accounts, keep old accounts open, and establish a long history with consistent and reliable payments, as well as a small "amount owed" in comparison to your income and credit limits.

It is possible for you to have a decent credit score or more than decent if you are willing to work towards it. Utilize family to start to gain new credit lines, if necessary. Make certain that if you are paying for something that uses credit to build your score, by putting the funds in your account, you are going home and paying that purchase off right away. It is only the steady, reliable, and consistent credit history that is going to offer a "great credit" appearance, as well as higher scores.

Since you have the tools available to you now, there is no better time than to get started right away with building great credit and increasing those scores.

As I have shown throughout this book, even a credit repair with moderate success can bring you countless benefits. All that matters is that you take the time to try. Suppose you go through this process and clear some issues; you only need to repeat it in a few years. The advantages of credit repair may take time to manifest, but by following all of the steps discussed in this book, you will definitely be able to clear your credit and increase your chances of receiving higher credit scores. It will also help you with finding a job, even though your credit is not entirely repaired. When someone is evaluating your credit report and sees the written statements and all the work you have put in the process, it shows how responsible and diligent you are about your finances and says a lot about who you are.

I hope that this book has not only convinced you about the benefits that come with repairing your credit but also that it has provided a simple and clear explanation of the steps you have to follow in order to do it successfully. I wanted to make credit repair accessible to everyone and suggest the best approach for a different number of problems. Many people become enthusiastic about credit repairing, and when they see the effort involved and the time required on the journey to good credit, they get discouraged and give up. Others give up after the first negative response from a creditor or credit report agency, and some even go through with it but stop doing things to improve their credit when they've finished the process and still haven't managed to fix all the negative items. Damage control is just as important as the process itself, and it has many future benefits. The important thing about the whole process is to stay motivated and continue improving.

So, what is next for you? The next step is to begin applying what you have learned in this eBook in your current situation and working as hard as you can to begin repairing your credit. What have you got to lose? Every day, even if you only take one step forward, you will be closer to your goal than you were the day before. It's the same way with anything else in life: you get what you put in. Best wishes to you!

The more valuable the business becomes to interested investors and other parties, the stronger the profile and the more depth there is in trade lines.

A good business credit profile and score can be built much more quickly than a business owner's credit profile. Furthermore, business credit approvals typically have higher dollar amounts than personal credit approvals.

Typically, business credit cards have higher credit limits. Multiple credit sources make it easier and faster to obtain approval.

Individual business credit approvals are also easier to obtain than consumer credit approvals for multiple credit cards or lines of credit.

These are some of the numerous advantages of establishing business credit for a company and its owner. Therefore, it is difficult for any business to be truly successful without first building a strong business credit profile and score and then leveraging it to grow.

You now have the know-how and tools you need to ensure that your company can establish and keep a good credit score and profile. Start building business credit for your company or using business credit to help you start a new business venture today with your newfound knowledge.

Once you've established a positive business credit profile, you can finally have the positive business credit and financial future you've always wanted.

CPSIA information can be obtained
at www.ICGtesting.com
Printed in the USA
BVHW090151220521
607889BV00010B/1600

9 781802 993363